The Notions of George Berkeley

Also available from Bloomsbury

Descartes and the Doubting Mind, by James Hill
Locke on Knowledge, Politics and Religion, edited by Kiyoshi Shimokawa and Peter R. Anstey
The Philosophy of Anne Conway, by Jonathan Head
The Evolution of Consciousness, by Paula Droege

The Notions of George Berkeley

Self, Substance, Unity and Power

James Hill

BLOOMSBURY ACADEMIC
LONDON • NEW YORK • OXFORD • NEW DELHI • SYDNEY

BLOOMSBURY ACADEMIC
Bloomsbury Publishing Plc
50 Bedford Square, London, WC1B 3DP, UK
1385 Broadway, New York, NY 10018, USA
29 Earlsfort Terrace, Dublin 2, Ireland

BLOOMSBURY, BLOOMSBURY ACADEMIC and the Diana logo are trademarks of
Bloomsbury Publishing Plc

First published in Great Britain 2022
This paperback edition published 2024

Copyright © James Hill, 2022

James Hill has asserted his right under the Copyright, Designs and Patents Act,
1988, to be identified as Author of this work.

For legal purposes the Acknowledgements on pp. viii–ix constitute an extension
of this copyright page.

Cover image: George Berkeley, 1685–1753, aka Bishop Berkeley (Bishop of Cloyne).
Anglo-Irish philosopher. After the painting by Vanderbank.
Classic Image / Alamy Stock Photo

All rights reserved. No part of this publication may be reproduced or transmitted in
any form or by any means, electronic or mechanical, including photocopying,
recording, or any information storage or retrieval system, without prior permission
in writing from the publishers.

Bloomsbury Publishing Plc does not have any control over, or responsibility for,
any third-party websites referred to or in this book. All internet addresses given in this
book were correct at the time of going to press. The author and publisher regret any
inconvenience caused if addresses have changed or sites have ceased to exist,
but can accept no responsibility for any such changes.

A catalogue record for this book is available from the British Library.

A catalog record for this book is available from the Library of Congress.

ISBN: HB: 978-1-3502-9968-9
PB: 978-1-3502-9972-6
ePDF: 978-1-3502-9969-6
eBook: 978-1-3502-9970-2

Typeset by Newgen KnowledgeWorks Pvt. Ltd., Chennai, India

To find out more about our authors and books visit www.bloomsbury.com
and sign up for our newsletters.

To Anna

The grand Mistake is that we think we have Ideas of the Operations of our Minds.

George Berkeley

Contents

Acknowledgements		viii
List of Abbreviations		x
1	Introduction	1
2	Berkeley's predecessors on self-knowledge	15
3	A notion of an active self	35
4	Notions and innatism	55
5	Sense perception: A passive or an active power?	71
6	Berkeley's conceptual dynamism	87
7	A notion of goodness	105
8	Number and the notion of God	115
Appendix		131
Notes		133
Bibliography		157
Index		165

Acknowledgements

I am grateful to audiences at the University of Neuchâtel, the Jagellonian University in Cracow, Trinity College Dublin, King's College London and the Czech Academy of Sciences in Prague for their responses to papers I have presented on Berkeley's notions at these various establishments. I am grateful to my colleagues and students at Charles University for our numerous discussions on and around the themes of this book over the last years, particularly Lukáš Kollert, Jakub Mihálik, Jindřich Karásek and Marina Barabas. The book has also benefitted greatly from the patient and penetrating questioning of Benjamin Hill, Benjamin Formanek, Alberto Lopez, James Mackey and Brad Thomson in a series of online, transatlantic, covid-defying seminars. I thank Stefan Storrie, who participated in these discussions too, and who also sent me detailed written criticisms which have corrected a range of blind spots and oversights. I thank Samuel Rickless for his penetrating comments in correspondence. I am grateful to Lilian Alweiss not only for her comments to the manuscript but also for our wider discussions on the nature of self-consciousness. I thank John Milton, who read draft versions of chapters, and whose encouragement and expertise have been immensely important to me over the years. Above all, let me thank David Berman for our many discussions and for giving me the benefit of his knowledge of Berkeley's life and work, as well as his own philosophical insight. While these friends and colleagues may not agree with all the conclusions that I come to, their open and critical voices have been an invaluable stimulus to the interpretation of Berkeley's notions and his philosophy of mind in the pages that follow. Let me finally thank the referees of Bloomsbury Press for their helpful critical observations.

Parts of this book have appeared in a different form elsewhere. In composing Chapters 5, 6 and 7, I have drawn on material from my articles 'The Synthesis of Empiricism and Innatism in Berkeley's Doctrine of Notions' and 'The Active Self and Perception in Berkeley's *Three Dialogues*'. For their kind permission in this respect, I would like to thank the editors of *Berkeley Studies*, where the first of these articles appeared (2010), and Stefan Storrie and Oxford University Press who edited and published *Berkeley's Three Dialogues: New Essays* (2018) in which the second article appeared. Finally, I would like to thank the Grant Agency of the Czech Republic (GAČR: P401/12/0833) for the support they have given me during the writing of this book.

Abbreviations

George Berkeley

Works	*The Works of George Berkeley, Bishop of Cloyne*, edited by A. A. Luce and T. E. Jessop. London: Nelson. 1947–53.
ALC	*Alciphron or the Minute Philosopher* (1732), *Works* III. (References are to dialogue, section and page number: e.g. ALC III, v, 298).
DHP	*Three Dialogues between Hylas and Philonous* (1713), *Works* II, pp. 163–263). (References are to dialogue and page number: e.g. DHP III, 231.)
DM	*De motu* (1721), *Works* IV, pp. 11–52 (Latin text with English translation by A. A. Luce). (References are to section number: e.g. DM §31.)
Notebooks	As 'Philosophical Commentaries', *Works* I, pp. 7–104. (References are to entry number.)
NTV	*An Essay towards a New Theory of Vision* (1709), *Works* I, pp. 159–239. (References are to section number: e.g. NTV §105.)
OWG	Sermon X, 'On the Will of God', *Works* VII, pp. 129–38. (References are to page number: e.g. OWG 130.)
PHK	*A Treatise concerning the Principles of Human Knowledge* (1710), *Works* II, pp. 19–113. (References are to section number: e.g. PHK §142.)
PO	*Passive Obedience* (1712), *Works* VI, pp. 13–46. (References are to section number: e.g. PO §12.)
Siris	*Siris: A Chain of Philosophical Reflexions and Inquiries concerning the Virtues of Tar-Water and divers other Subjects connected together and arising One from Another* (1744), *Works* V, pp. 25–164. (References are to section number: e.g. *Siris* §308.)

TVV	*The Theory of Vision Vindicated and Explained* (1733), *Works* I, pp. 249–76. (References are to section number: e.g. TVV §24.)

René Descartes

AT	*Oeuvres de Descartes*, edited by Charles Adam and Paul Tannery, Paris: Vrin, 1996. (References are to volume and page number: e.g. AT VII 35.)
CSM	*The Philosophical Writings of Descartes*, translated by John Cottingham, Robert Stoothoff and Dugald Murdoch, Cambridge: Cambridge University Press, 1985. (References are to volume and page number: e.g. CSM II 17.)

David Hume

T	*A Treatise of Human Nature*, edited by L. A. Selby-Bigge, with revisions by P. H. Nidditch. Oxford: Clarendon, 1978. (References are to page number: e.g. T 174.)
E	*Enquiries Concerning Human Understanding and Concerning the Principles of Morals*, edited by L. A. Selby-Bigge, with revisions by P. H. Nidditch. Oxford: Clarendon, 1975. (References are to page number: e.g. E 6.)

John Locke

Drafts	Drafts for the Essay Concerning Human Understanding, and Other Philosophical Writings, edited by Peter H. Nidditch and G. A. J. Rogers, Volume 1: Drafts A and B, Oxford: Oxford University Press, 1990.
Essay	*An Essay Concerning Human Understanding*, edited by Peter H. Nidditch. Oxford: Clarendon Press, 1975. (References are to book, chapter, section and page numbers: e.g. E.II.xxiii.15, p. 305.)

Examination	*An Examination of P. Malebranche's Opinion of Seeing All Things in God*, in *The Works of John Locke Esq*, London, 1714, volume III, pp. 429–50.
Corres	*The Correspondence of John Locke*, edited by Esmond de Beer, 8 volumes. Oxford: Oxford University Press, 1976–89. (References are to volume number, letter number and page: e.g. Corres. 4, L 1544, p. 533.)

Immanuel Kant

CPR	*The Critique of Pure Reason*, translated by Norman Kemp Smith. London: Macmillan, 1933. (References are to page number to the first and second editions of the German original: e.g. A417/B444.)

1

Introduction

One might divide George Berkeley's philosophical work into two fundamental projects. The first is that of persuading his readers of the soundness of his 'immaterial hypothesis'[1] – the negative claim that material substance does not exist. Immaterialism exercises Berkeley's considerable argumentative skills as he provides many different reasons for treating matter as not only an unnecessary or empty category, but – more strongly – as suffering from internal contradiction. This project includes his denial of abstract ideas, his views on linguistic meaning and his delimitation of the representative power of ideas, all of which are primarily motivated by the denial of matter. It also includes his defence of immaterialism on the principles of 'common sense'. It is this strand in Berkeley's thinking that takes pride of place in his *Principles* and the *Three Dialogues*, and it is the part of his work that made him famous – or infamous – among his contemporaries, and which receives most attention in the literature today.

Alongside the polemical attack on matter and materialism, however, is a second, positive project. Berkeley seeks to establish a defensible metaphysical picture of the world in the absence of matter. Central to this positive endeavour is a conception of the nature of the mind, along with conceptions of the fundamental ontological categories of substance, unity and causation. This positive project also includes answers to the questions of how the mind becomes aware of itself and its acts, and of how it gains knowledge of other minds including the divine active principle that, in Berkeley's view, directs and sustains the phenomenal world. It is in addressing these epistemological questions that Berkeley develops his doctrine of 'notions' which is the subject of this monograph.

The doctrine of notions explains how mind with its different operations – its substance-hood, unity and its causality – are known to us. Berkeley's use of the term 'notion' indicates his dissatisfaction with the widespread tendency in the 'New Philosophy' of his day to characterize knowledge of the inner sphere as mediated by 'ideas'. Berkeley introduced the term 'notion' in the narrow sense that distinguishes it from 'idea', in his 1734 editions of the *Principles* and the *Three Dialogues*. However, this relatively late terminological innovation did not mark a doctrinal change. Berkeley had, in his earlier writings, already rejected the view that it is by the representative power of ideas that we have knowledge of the inner sphere. Indeed, such a rejection is visible as early as his Notebooks, and the first edition of the *Principles* of 1710 was crystal clear on this point. While nominally introduced in 1734, then, the doctrine of notions is in fact a part of his system from the first period of his philosophy.[2]

We shall examine, in Chapter 2, how some of the most influential thinkers on Berkeley's early philosophy – Hobbes, Malebranche and Locke – had denied that immediate knowledge of mind, or spiritual substance, was attainable at all, and, in Chapter 3, we shall see how Berkeley, with his doctrine of notions, sought to vindicate immediate knowledge of the active, spiritual, self. We shall examine how exactly self-knowledge is achievable, in Berkeley's view, and why he insists on our rejecting the easy, and seemingly natural, locution that we have an 'idea of the mind'. Knowledge of the mind, Berkeley argues, is not to be treated as in any parallel way to the perceptual knowledge of objects, and thus cannot be captured by the contemplation of an idea or representation, particularly not one perceived by an 'inner sense' when construed on analogy with the outer senses.

Berkeley's account of our knowledge of the mind will be examined in Chapters 3 and 4, and we will see that it also becomes the pathway to a proper grasp of the primary ontological categories of substance and causality. These categories, he holds, must be understood through the direct knowledge we have of our own active mind and its acts – the species of knowledge that he refers to as 'notions'.

Furthermore, our own essentially active nature allows us, on Berkeley's view, to understand the divine mind which takes the place of inert material substance as the source of our perceptions, as discussed in Chapter 8. It is also reflected in his positive account of conceptual thought, discussed in Chapter 6, according to which concepts are treated as things we *do* rather than things we *perceive*, and therefore necessarily draw on notions as well as ideas.

Of course, the negative and positive projects that we have outlined are not fully independent of one another but are rather mutually supportive in Berkeley's philosophy. A proper recognition of the nature of mind or spirit allows Berkeley's opposition to the existence of matter to become a serious and natural proposition. One reason why Berkeley rejects any role for an inert material substance is because he finds that causal power can be fully understood in terms of mental acts. The mind is the causal foundation of the world of things that we perceive. Such a view, one should note, had already been anticipated in the Scholastic and Cartesian doctrine that the world lacks the power to continue in existence without the active support of God. As Berkeley himself stresses, the world in his idealism is no more inert and lacking in self-sustaining power than the material world described by Descartes in which matter is dependent on continuous divine conservation.[3]

Our task of making sense of Berkeley's doctrine of notions, and his philosophy of mind in general, will only be successful if we recognize an important obstacle that stands in its way. There is an entrenched reading which treats Berkeley as belonging to one side of the empiricist–rationalist divide. I believe it is the widespread perception that Berkeley is an empiricist that has often thwarted attempts to make proper sense of his conception of mind and of self-knowledge, and indeed of the whole of the second project outlined above. The empiricist reading will be examined in detail below, particularly in Chapters 4, 5 and 8, but let me now make an initial sketch of its fundamental features.

The empiricist paradigm

The interpretation of Berkeley's philosophical work that has been dominant since the middle of the nineteenth century treats Berkeley as the second great British empiricist and as the philosopher who stands between, and connects, the work of Locke and Hume. I shall call this interpretation the 'empiricist paradigm'.

I find it useful to treat the empiricist reading as a *paradigm* because it has a holistic structure of theses and assumptions that makes it almost impervious to piecemeal criticism. To question this interpretation, it is never enough to point to anomalies – recalcitrant statements or passages – because the empiricist reading is able to neutralize their impact by telling us they are elliptical or 'tactical' or, in certain cases, by downplaying the importance of the text in which they appear.

I also call the empiricist reading a paradigm because I want to stress its historical character. It arose in a particular period, and since then it has been supported by the institutional practice of philosophy – particularly by how Berkeley is taught and how he is categorized by journals and libraries. But I shall not attempt to describe this historical and sociological dimension of the empiricist interpretation – I trust the reader will be already familiar with it, and that its presence need not be detailed or demonstrated.

Let me confine myself to a few brief comments about the history of this interpretational paradigm. It was first established by the Hegelian school, then maintained and refined by British empiricist thinkers of the twentieth century, and today it remains the default framework for understanding Berkeley. We find expression of the paradigm, in embryonic form, in the 'Lectures on the History of Philosophy' that were delivered by Hegel in Jena and published after his death.[4] Hegel's conviction that Berkeley 'proceeds from the standpoint of Locke' is then taken up by Kuno Fischer, Wilhelm Windelband and other German historians of philosophy of the latter part of the nineteenth century.[5] In England, it was made popular by the T. H. Green, a follower of Hegel, in his 'Introduction' to Hume's *Philosophical Works*.[6] It was espoused with particular verve and wit by Bertrand Russell,[7] and it is also a fundamental part of the popular interpretations of A. J. Ayer and J. O. Urmson.[8] But its influence and expression goes far beyond the handful of thinkers I have just named. The empiricist reading remains the established view today, often providing the implicit framework for interpretations of Berkeley in scholarly work. It makes four large claims.

Firstly, and most importantly, Berkeley is treated as a concept empiricist. He is thus seen as part of a tradition of empiricism in which John Locke is the most significant forerunner. Berkeley 'proceeds directly from' the standpoint of Locke, Hegel declares.[9] While Berkeley may have disagreed with Locke on important issues, relating particularly to ontology, it is still thought that he was working within the same epistemological framework, and that his thought was thus in principle opposed to the Cartesian rationalist tradition.

Concept empiricism can be encapsulated in the scholastic maxim: *nihil est in intellectu quod non prius fuerit in sensu*. In accordance with this, it rejects the possibility of innate content in the mind and excludes any appeal to a faculty, such as the 'pure intellect', with access to content underived from sense experience. This interpretation thus treats Berkeley as siding, in so far as epistemology is concerned, with Gassendi, Hobbes and Locke, and against Descartes, Spinoza, Malebranche and Leibniz.

The second claim of the empiricist interpretation of Berkeley is that his famous critique and rejection of material substance leads, almost inevitably, to David Hume's rejection of spiritual substance. This claim has been advanced in a stronger form, such that Berkeley had already, covertly, endorsed the Humean move.[10] But usually the claim is more circumspect. Berkeley's rejection of material substance, along with his maintenance of spiritual substance, is held to be a philosophically precarious position – a leaning tower that soon falls when Hume brings pressure to bear on it. Interpreters thus treat Hume's famous view of the mind in his *Treatise*, according to which it is nothing more than a 'bundle of perceptions', as the natural extension of Berkeley's critique of material substance. T. H. Green wrote that

> in his zeal against matter [Berkeley] took away the ground from under the spiritualism which he sought to maintain. He simply invited a successor in speculation, of colder blood than himself, to try the solution of spirit in the same crucible with matter.[11]

Or, as A. J. Ayer puts it:

> Berkeley had eliminated matter, at least as the physicists conceived it, but left minds intact. Hume, an avowed sceptic, showed that this favouritism was unjustified.[12]

Of course, this second claim about the relation between the philosophy of Berkeley and Hume is not exclusive to proponents of the empiricist paradigm. Thomas Reid, in the late eighteenth century, had seen Berkeley and Hume as philosophical brothers-in-arms, with Hume extending a sceptical attack that had been started by Berkeley and other proponents of what he called the 'theory of ideas'. Yet Reid did not develop an empiricist reading because he thought that Berkeley and Hume were working out the sceptical implications of a premise that all early modern philosophers since Descartes – empiricist and rationalist alike – had signed up to: 'We can have no conception of anything but what resembles some idea in our minds.'[13]

The third claim of the empiricist interpretation is usually made by implication rather than by straightforward assertion. It is that Berkeley's doctrine of notions, which accounts for the self-knowledge of spirit, is a problematic and evasive part of his thought that, as it stands, is of only marginal significance. Berkeley's distinction between ideas and notions is either treated as a merely terminological issue or dismissed as too sketchy to be worth expounding in detail. Interpreters therefore lament Berkeley's failure to publish the Second Part of the *Principles*, in which, it seems, this doctrine would have been properly set forth.[14]

When the doctrine of notions has become the focus of inquiry it has typically been thought in need of very extensive reconstruction. In the one book-length study of Berkeley's doctrine of notions, Daniel Flage, committed to the empiricist reading, interpreted Berkeley's discussion of notions through the lens of semantic theory developed in twentieth-century analytical philosophy. He defended the thesis that, for Berkeley, we do not know our own minds and its actions immediately, or 'by acquaintance', but only 'by description'.[15] Such a conclusion seems to run counter to Berkeley's own explicit statements that we have 'immediate' and 'intuitive' knowledge of our own selves,[16] and, as I will show, it renders the most interesting part of his philosophy of spirit obscure and lacking in coherence.[17]

A fourth and final claim – which is again usually made by implication rather than by explicit assertion – concerns the development of Berkeley's philosophy. It is thought that Berkeley's early philosophical view remained unchanged until, late in life, he published *Siris* (1744). This last philosophical work is thought to constitute a significant change of orientation, occasioned perhaps by a serious decline in his philosophical powers. It is widely held that *Siris* can be safely set aside and ignored. As a result, Berkeley's philosophical heritage is treated as contained in his early works, which are read as if he had written them – along with important changes in editions as late as 1734 – in a single burst of philosophical creativity.

It is by no means coincidental, of course, that *Siris* is treated so harshly by the empiricist paradigm. In *Siris* Berkeley's favourable view of Platonist and rationalist doctrine is most explicit. If this work was to be included in Berkeley's philosophical legacy, then the first claim of the traditional interpretation – that Berkeley's philosophical thought is founded on concept empiricism – would have to be at least seriously questioned. When *Siris* is mentioned, it is often described as if it lacked any philosophical content. George Pitcher, for example, writes that '*Siris* begins as a tract about tar-water, and then passes on through chemistry and cosmology to religion'.[18] The implication that the philosophical discussions of the nature of spirit, of the intellect, of knowledge and of number that occupy Berkeley, particularly in the final eighty (or so) sections of *Siris*, can be passed off as either 'cosmology' or 'religion' suggests a highly unconventional conception of those two fields.

In this book I shall question the empiricist paradigm for interpreting Berkeley, and I shall put forward opposing views on all these four main points. But I do not wish to deny that there is *real* justification for the orthodox reading, and that the four claims I have described do have *real* grounding in historical fact. My objection to the empiricist paradigm is rather that it is one-sided. It throws light on only a part of Berkeley's philosophy, obscuring as much of his thought as it illuminates. Above all, I believe that the empiricist reading cannot make sense of the most fundamental distinction, lying at the heart of Berkeley's philosophy, the distinction between ideas and spirits. This distinction is so clear-cut, especially in Berkeley's early works, that it has been described, by David Berman, as Berkeley's 'dualism'.[19]

Berkeley's dualism

We are certainly more accustomed to seeing the term 'dualism' applied to Descartes' split between matter and mind. Indeed, the term dualism has often been used in the literature as a synonym for substantial dualism. Berkeley, who thought that material substance did not exist, is thus usually treated as a monist rather than a dualist. This is harmless enough if substantial dualism is understood. But, when Berkeley distinguishes between the active spiritual substance and its passive ideas, he makes a split which is arguably more radical than Descartes' substantial dualism. After all, the two finite substances in Descartes' philosophy – matter and mind – have quite a lot in common from a metaphysical point of view. They mirror one another in ontological structure, each grounding a single main attribute that is modified by a variety of modes. Berkeley's ideas and spirits, on the other hand, are utterly unalike.

Certainly, there is a relation of mutual dependency between ideas and spirits. Ideas cannot exist without perceiving spirits, and finite spirits cannot operate without ideas. We are not talking of two self-contained substances as in the Cartesian system. But the mutual relatedness of spirit and idea does not stop Berkeley's dualism being a 'stark bifurcation of being', as Roberts has called it:[20]

> *Thing* or *being* is the most general name of all, it comprehends under it two kinds entirely distinct and heterogeneous, and which have nothing common but the name, to wit, *spirits* and *ideas*.[21]

And Berkeley confirms towards the end of the *Principles* that the ontological divide corresponds to an epistemological divide:

> Spirits and ideas are things so wholly different, that when we say, they exist, *they are known*, or the like, these words must not be thought to signify anything common to both natures. There is nothing alike or common in them.[22]

Now, this book takes these statements seriously. Berkeley urges us to recognize not only the ontological heterogeneity of spirits and ideas, but also their epistemological heterogeneity. They are known in utterly divergent ways. The difference from Descartes is again noteworthy. Descartes' substantial dualism does not bring with it a fundamental epistemological division. True, the mind is known first by those who reason 'in an orderly way'. But Descartes finds that knowledge of matter, once attained, is the work of the same faculty – the pure intellect – that gives us knowledge of the mind. What is more, we have an *idea* of material substance just as we have an *idea* of the mind, or *res cogitans*. Both species of knowledge are treated by Descartes as the objects of clear and distinct intellectual 'perception'.

Berkeley's dualism of idea and spirit asserts – in contrast to Descartes – that our knowledge is gained in two utterly distinct ways. This leads Berkeley to abandon the Cartesian use of the same language of ideas for both the corporeal and spiritual spheres because he thinks that it papers over this fundamental epistemological divide. Certainly, Berkeley allows that we may not always be free to determine our terminology unless 'the world will have it so',[23] but in his own writings he consistently refused to use the word 'idea' to describe our immediate knowledge of spirit, and, from 1734, uses the term 'notion' in this respect.

This dualism means that we must contrast Berkeley not only with the Cartesian tradition, but also with early modern empiricism. Despite its different disputes with rationalism, the empiricism of Locke still accepted the Cartesian perceptual model of cognition, with its broad use of the term 'idea' for all the immediate objects of knowledge, including those of the inner sphere. Locke gives us the internal sense of reflection which perceives our own mental operations, furnishing the mind with ideas of them. Berkeley's rejection of this internal sense, and his advocacy of a non-perceptual approach to spiritual knowledge, marks a departure from Locke that is at least as significant as anything the two philosophers held in common.

My aim here will be to steer a middle course when it comes to interpreting Berkeley with relation to the empiricist–rationalist divide. On the one hand, the ontological and epistemological distinction between spirits and ideas will make much better sense to us if we treat his account of our knowledge of spirits as akin to (though never identical with) the doctrine of innatism. While, on the other hand, we need to see how the empiricist *nihil est in intellectu* principle is applicable to Berkeley's account of ideas, or the passive objects of perception. As a first approximation we might then say that Berkeley's doctrine of notions shows an affinity to rationalism, while his account of ideas is empiricist.

If we keep Berkeley's dualism in mind we will appreciate how Hume's critique of spiritual substance – which seeks a *perception* of spiritual substance – misconstrued Berkeley's account of spirit (if it was indeed meant as a critique of that account), something I hope to show in Chapter 3. We will also see why *Siris* offers us reflection on his earlier thought about spirit that develops themes already present in his philosophy. Although the philosophical sections of *Siris* should not be thought of as constituting the lost second part of the *Principles*, they do give us mature reflection on some of the themes that the missing manuscript would have dealt with. Overall, I hope to show how Berkeley's account of spirit, and of our awareness of the spiritual sphere, was highly original and that it led him to depart from the assumptions which had made the empiricist–rationalist divide so pronounced.

A developmental framework

Now, if Berkeley's thinking about mind develops over his writing career, then we need to establish a straightforward way of referring to the stages in that development. I shall adopt a relatively loose three-part framework. Though what Berkeley says about the mind and its notions is often expanded between consecutive publications, such as the *Principles* and the *Three Dialogues*, we may delineate three broad stages in the Berkeley's reflection on spirit.

(1) The Heroic Period (1707–21). David Berman originally used the term 'heroic period' to refer to the publication of the *Principles* and *Three Dialogues* in the years 1710 to 1713.[24] This is the key episode in a more general early period which extends both backwards, to include the Notebooks (1707–8) and *Essay on Vision* (1709), as well as forwards to include *De motu* (1721). In this first phase, Berkeley's published thought about spirit is restricted to fundamentals. The core of the doctrine is certainly visible, but it is somewhat isolated from his main preoccupation with the denial of matter. This period includes the writing of Berkeley's lost manuscript of the second part to his *Principles* that would have dealt in more detail with spirit as well as with ethics. *De motu*, the first work Berkeley published after this loss, contains perhaps some indications of what went into the lost draft.[25]

(2) The Middle Period (1731–4). This second stage is constituted by the publishing activity in the years after Berkeley's return to the British Isles at the end of 1731, following his frustrated efforts to establish a school in Bermuda. Berkeley now strengthens the place of notions in his thought, adding passages to the editions of the *Principles* and *Three Dialogues* of 1734 that establish the narrow use of the term 'notion' which we are concerned with. He also explicitly claims that relations are known not by idea but by notion – a move that Alexander Fraser described as a 'germ of Kantism'.[26] This phase also includes the apologetical dialogue *Alciphron* in which Berkeley is more expansive in his approach to ethical concepts, and expresses his opposition to those philosophers (Shaftesbury and Hutcheson) who claim that we owe our knowledge of the Good to a peculiar 'sense'.

(3) The Final Period (1734–53). The final phase of the development of Berkeley's philosophy of spirit is contained in *Siris* (1744). It is

characterized by a systematic attempt to merge his doctrine of notions with Plato's *Ideas*, which had in his view been subjected to a 'monstrous representation' by Aristotle and his followers.[27] In this final phase, notions have taken centre stage in his discussions of the mind and the divine nature, and he now openly disparages ideas as 'the fleeting, transient objects of sense'.[28] Likewise, Berkeley clarifies and broadens his opposition to the Aristotelian concept of substance with its assumption that accidents require a 'substrate'.

One will notice that the second and third phases are relatively close to one another in time, with only ten years separating the new editions of the *Principles* and *Three Dialogues* of 1734, on the one hand, and the publication of *Siris* in 1744, on the other. In fact, the temporal proximity may be yet closer as the philosophy of *Siris* had probably ripened in Berkeley's mind in the decade preceding its publication. We should not, therefore, be surprised if features of the Middle Period already anticipate the last neo-Platonic phase.

More generally, the developmental story that I wish to present is marked by overall continuity. There are no outright denials of previous doctrine. Instead, we find Berkeley filling in and extending what he had said in earlier works. Like a painter who first makes a sketch before returning to it to introduce detail and colour, and perhaps an occasional modification, Berkeley in the two later periods adds more developed doctrine to the remarks made about spirit in the heroic period. But it is recognisably the same picture.[29]

A coincidence of opposites

Let us now return to the overall view of the mind or spirit that develops over these three periods. As I have said, the aim of this book is not to deny the empiricist reading *tout court*, even in the final stage of the development. I am not seeking to prove that Berkeley belonged to the 'other side', as one of the rationalist opponents of empiricism. Such an innatist reading was defended by Henry Bracken, who regarded Berkeley not as a British empiricist, but 'an Irish Cartesian'.[30] It is tempting to say that the innatist reading 'goes too far'. In one sense, this is true because it ignores the empiricist element in Berkeley's thought that undeniably exists, and which is particularly apparent in his critique of material substance. It switches Berkeley's allegiance from one camp to the other, recognizing no third way.

Really, however, the innatist reading does not go far enough. We should not forget that contraries are only opposed to one another insofar as they fall under the same class. To see Berkeley as an innatist or rationalist is to accept that his philosophy belongs to the 'new way of ideas'. Such an interpretation fails to appreciate Berkeley's dissatisfaction with this whole framework when he argued – just as forcefully in the Heroic Period as in the later periods – that the inner sphere is not known to us by ideas, nor by any kind of perception.

I shall argue that Berkeley sought to reject the perceptual model for self-knowledge, and indeed for the inner sphere per se. As we shall see, his immediate predecessors and his contemporaries routinely assumed that to know oneself meant to somehow *perceive* oneself. Sometimes the perception in question was of a quasi-sensory kind delivered by inner sense; sometimes it was a perception of the intellect, working independently of sense; sometimes it was even held that the relevant perception was humanly inaccessible, but present in the mind of God. Despite the diversity of these views, all of them agreed that knowledge of spirit, to the extent that it is attainable, is achieved by a special perception of our own selves, or of our states or activities. It is this assumption of mainstream early modern philosophy that Berkeley wholeheartedly rejects.[31]

In this book, I shall argue that by breaking with the 'new way of ideas' on this point, and by abandoning the perceptual model of cognition in his treatment of spirit, Berkeley is able to combine the insights of both empiricism and innatism. He does this without diluting the two doctrines or blending them in a compromise solution. He recognizes and respects both poles, reconciling them with one another. Berkeley shows us how we may assert the empiricist principle *nihil est in intellectu quod non fuerit in sensu*, and yet, at the same time, recognize, with the rationalists, that our knowledge of substance, of unity, of causation – and of a host of other intellectual elements – is not derived from sense experience at all.

This marriage of the two perspectives can, I think, be usefully described as a 'coincidence of opposites'.[32] By this I mean that Berkeley is not simply seeking a middle position, or an Aristotelian mean, between two extremes. Nor is he being eclectic, juxtaposing disparate doctrines. Rather he came to think each side has lighted upon a distinct truth and that these truths when properly understood are mutually supportive. The point is to embrace both truths at once by applying them to the different but complementary sides of the idea–spirit dualism.

If 'the owl of Minerva takes wing at dusk', it should not surprise us that this reconciliation is most clearly expressed by Berkeley in his last work, *Siris*:

> [Aristotle] held that the mind of man was a *tabula rasa*, and that there were no innate ideas. Plato, on the contrary, held original ideas in the mind; that is, notions which never were or can be in the sense, such as being, beauty, goodness, likeness, parity. Some, perhaps, may think the truth to be this: that there are properly no *ideas*, or passive objects, in the mind but what were derived from sense: but that there are also besides these her own acts or operations; such are *notions*.[33]

In this passage, Aristotle stands for the empiricist tradition, as is suggested by the reference to the *tabula rasa*, and the allusion to the *nihil est in intellectu* principle. Plato, on the other hand, stands for the innatist tradition, in which there are 'original ideas in the mind'. The important point for us is that Berkeley sees his dualism as incorporating these two opposing views. Aristotle and the latter-day empiricists are right in so far as ideas, or the objects of mental perception, are concerned – there are, indeed, no passive mental objects that are underived from sense or that sit in the mind from its very inception. But Berkeley also recognizes the truth which Plato and the innatists draw our attention to. The mind does include more than sense-based ideas because its acts and operations are native to it, and these amount to 'notions', providing us with a second kind of direct knowledge. Berkeley seeks to show how the elements of intellectual thought – particularly those dearest to the rationalist philosophers – are best understood as our own activities. They are not ideas, to be peered at by a mental eye, but rather the mind's 'own acts or operations'. These original *notions*, as we shall see, are constituted by what the intellect *does* with the different ideas that it perceives.

2

Berkeley's predecessors on self-knowledge

What is the thinking, conscious self? This is a question that no systematic philosopher can avoid. But that does not mean that a clear-cut positive answer to the question must be given. One response is to say that the real nature of the self or mind is obscure or even quite unknowable. This sceptical response was well-represented among Berkeley's immediate predecessors. It was given in different forms by Malebranche and Locke. Hobbes too, though he embraced a mechanical explanation of the mind, was certainly sceptical of any reflective knowledge of a spiritual self. These different expressions of scepticism about true self-knowledge were a source of dismay to Berkeley. He thought that they were symptomatic of a defective approach to the inner sphere.

In this chapter, we will explore the views of the four thinkers whose view on self-cognition would have been most familiar to Berkeley: Descartes, Hobbes, Malebranche and Locke. It should be borne in mind that we elucidate these thinkers from Berkeley's own point of view, highlighting aspects of their thought that he would have found significant or controversial. In Chapter 4, we shall turn to Berkeley's critique of these accounts of self-reflection.

Descartes and the perceptual model of cognition

Descartes was not one to profess scepticism when it came to the nature of the self. Knowledge of the mind, self or soul – Descartes uses these terms synonymously – was foundational to his metaphysics. The self is the first thing that is known by a philosopher who proceeds in 'an orderly way', and it marks the point of departure for the construction and proof of his system. On this question there was a clear divide between Descartes and the scholastics, for whom self-knowledge was a derivative sort of knowledge, arrived at by analogy with our knowledge of external objects. For Descartes external objects provide no help in the quest for self-knowledge. Self-knowledge is attainable even if we look upon our experience of the external world as a mere dream. It is analytically prior to knowledge of external things, and it constitutes the exemplary case of certain knowledge, or of what Descartes calls a 'clear and distinct perception'.

Central to Descartes's account of self-knowledge is his claim that we have an *idea* of the self. One cannot begin to understand what he says about self-awareness without appreciating his innovative use of this term 'idea'. Descartes knew that the term had traditionally been used – by Christian Platonists – to refer to intellectual forms in the mind of God. But it was a term that he wished to bring down from the heavens and to apply to all the objects of thought and knowledge in finite human minds. This new understanding of idea was adopted by others and Descartes's work signalled the beginning of what Edward Stillingfleet called the 'new way of ideas', so characteristic of early modern philosophy.

What is an idea? Descartes was challenged on his unusual employment of 'idea' by Thomas Hobbes in the Third Set of Objections to the *Meditations*. In response, Descartes defined his most important technical term as follows:

> I am taking the word 'idea' to refer to whatever is immediately perceived by the mind [*immediate à mente percipitur*].[1]

This definition leans, quite explicitly, on the concept of perception, and it naturally prompts the further question of what 'perception' itself signifies. On this point, however, Descartes is less forthcoming, and no explicit definition of perception is put forward in his writings. Indeed, the term 'perception' (*perceptio*) is so fundamental to Descartes's philosophy, and its meaning is presupposed in so many different passages, that it would probably be hard to elucidate it without simultaneously setting forth the whole system. But we can at least make some comments.

One thing is obvious: when Descartes talks of 'perception' he is not just talking of sense perception, even when that includes sensory images in the memory or imagination. Rather, perception is taken to mean any receptive state of cognition. He is at pains to show that there are purely intellectual perceptions that lack any sensory ingredient. Among these are the perceptions of the simple notions of metaphysics as well as of geometrical entities, such as point, line and triangle, which cannot be depicted in the images of the corporeal imagination, although *inadequate* images of these things may be entertained.

Perception does not refer even primarily to sense perception. Rather it is these purely intellectual acts of perception that are to be treated as paradigmatic when we think about Cartesian perception. The images of sense perception, which involve the body, are taken to be inferior, 'impure' perceptions. Having said that, sensory perception may, unofficially, play a larger role. After all, Descartes couches his presentation of intellectual perception in the language of vision. His guiding analogy is one of light, and a mental organ of sight is often implicitly assumed. Thus, when Descartes tells us (in the definition of idea above) that ideas are perceived '*by the mind*', the mind would seem to be a kind of 'fleshless eye'.[2] While intellectual vision is meant to be the primary form of perception, the physical sense of sight may still work as the unconscious model that Descartes draws upon when making intellectual vision perspicuous to himself and his readers.

Descartes on self-cognition

Now Descartes uses his perceptual model of cognition to make sense of self-knowledge.[3] The mind knows itself by having a perception, or idea, of itself. This idea is one of pure intellect, which is only possible when we draw off the veil of sensory imagery that normally occupies our attention.[4]

> I ... realise that none of the things that the imagination enables me to grasp is at all relevant to this knowledge of myself which I possess, and that the mind must therefore be more carefully diverted from such things if it is to perceive [*ut percipiat*] its own nature as distinctly as possible.[5]

Let us look a little closer at what Descartes says about this perception of the self in other places. As previously remarked, he frequently couches self-awareness in the language of vision, using a systematic analogy with the eye. He writes, for example, of how the meditator 'turns his mind's eye upon himself' to directly perceive an idea of his own mind.[6] Indeed, the turning of the mind's eye onto the mind itself is an analogy that Descartes calls up in numerous places to illuminate self-knowledge.

Pierre Gassendi was quick to point out a fundamental problem in this analogy, writing:

> The faculty itself, not being outside itself, cannot transmit a semblance of itself to itself, and hence cannot produce any awareness of itself or, in other words, cannot perceive itself. ... The eye can see itself in a mirror, but it cannot see itself in itself.[7]

Descartes's response to this objection is to disavow any analogy with the physical process of vision at all. The perception of the mind is unique and *sui generis*. In fact, it underlies all corporeal perception, and thus enables sense perception itself, since the mind is the only real perceiver. The sense of sight is, then, really made possible by a perception of the mind:

> It is ... easy to answer this by saying that it is not the eye which sees the mirror rather than itself, but the mind alone which recognizes the mirror, the eye and itself.[8]

So, Descartes's official position, stated when his talk of mental vision is subject to criticism, is that we cannot begin to understand the perception of the mind by making observations about any form of sensory perception, including visual perception. But whether Descartes can really stand by this official disavowal is another matter. It seems to render his use of the term 'perception' systematically confusing, for if there is no good analogy between perception by sense and mental perception, then the word 'perception' may be little more than a misleading homonym in these two applications. What's more, if the specifically visual metaphor is a mere *façon de parler*, one might wonder why it is used so often by Descartes and thought to be so apt.

Descartes wishes to be understood quite literally when he says that we have a clear and distinct idea of the mind, perceived by only the mind itself. Yet, this claim is fraught with paradox even if we ignore the analogy with sight. Any perception, after all, would seem to involve a separation of subject and object. But such a separation would surely thwart the act of self-perception. The perceptual model of the mind's self-knowledge suggests that we can survey our own nature, and yet at the same time capture the subject of that surveying.

An infinite regress threatens, with an indefinite series of mental acts each perceiving its predecessor. As we will see, it is this kind of worry that seems to occupy Berkeley in his critique of the perceptual model in the *Principles*.[9]

The threat to Descartes's account is intensified by two other specific views that are usually attributed to him. Firstly, he seems to hold that all thinking – and by that he means all mental activity – is conscious.[10] If this is so, it would mean that the infinite regress we have mentioned is a live problem. For if an unconscious mental act had been possible then the regress might have been halted by our positing a mental act of self-perception that was unconscious to the self. But where unconscious mental activity is ruled out, an act of self-consciousness, *qua* thought, will always require a further act of perception, and so on *ad infinitum*.[11]

A second problem, which would have been acutely apparent to Berkeley, arises from Descartes's split between active and passive faculties of the mind. When we come to the purely active thoughts of the mind, typified by willing, and by the volitional component in judgement (and perhaps also by the emotions) it is not clear how they could be known by the perception of an idea. And yet Descartes tells us, on different occasions, that *all* the objects of our thoughts are ideas, acts of the will not excepted. Descartes responds to Hobbes's probing on this matter as follows:

> When I want something, or am afraid of something, I simultaneously perceive that I want, or am afraid; and this is why I count volition and fear among my ideas.[12]

Here Descartes seems to be positing two parallel mental processes. For every act of will there is, at the very same time, a perception of that act. The passive perception of our volitions accompanies those volitions in an inner duet. Descartes talks here as if the coincidence of the two mental events – volition and perception of the volition – was universal, but not founded on any *necessary* inner connection. Really, however, the perceptions of volition must have a necessary bond to the volitions perceived for, as we have just indicated, unconscious mental activity of any sort, including volition, seems to have been ruled out in principle.

A further vulnerability in this account of our knowledge of volition, and other mental activity, is that it fails to explain how I *own* my volitions. One might ask why the act of will perceived is felt to be *my* activity. If it is made conscious to me by my perception of it, then it threatens to become only a mere event that occurs within me, not an act of mine produced by my agency. The Cartesian account seems to have me peering at my volitions to discover when they occur and what exactly they dictate. But that would hardly seem necessary if I were their inner motive force.

Perhaps it is for these reasons that Descartes, in his last work *The Passions of the Soul*, published in 1649, shows dissatisfaction with the perceptual model for understanding volition. In Section 19, he begins by reasserting the broad position he had espoused in reply to Hobbes:

> It is certain that we cannot will anything without thereby perceiving that we are willing it. And although willing something is an action with respect to our soul, the perception of such willing may be said to be a passion in the soul.

Then, however, he is inclined to fuse these active and passive components together:

> But because this perception is really one and the same thing as the volition, and names are always determined by whatever is most noble, we do not normally call it a 'passion', but solely an 'action'.[13]

The perception of the willing seems, in this passage, to have become an aspect of the act of will itself. This would suggest that the term 'perception', and its conceptual twin, 'idea', have become redundant, and even misleading, when applied to the mind's acts of will. Perhaps Descartes is indicating here that he no longer finds the perceptual model of self-awareness adequate. If this is so, then Berkeley's account of self-awareness, that we shall examine in the chapters that follow, might be seen as arising from Descartes's own discomfort with the perceptual model he had introduced and made so popular.[14]

Hobbes: 'The soul is something of which we have no idea at all'

We know, from his Notebooks, that Berkeley paid attention to the views of Thomas Hobbes. Hobbes was a materialist, and a reputed atheist. This made him one of Berkeley's natural adversaries, standing alongside Spinoza and the 'free-thinkers', such as John Toland and Anthony Collins. Berkeley seems to have been primarily acquainted with Hobbes's thought by reading the trenchant critique of Descartes's *Meditations* in the Third Set of Objections.[15]

Central to Hobbes's Objections is a root-and-branch rejection of Descartes's account of spiritual substance. I wish to focus on this negative part of Hobbes's thought because – strange as it may seem – Berkeley's doctrine of notions shows that he recognized its soundness. Hobbes's critical approach to Descartes also found an echo, in succeeding years, in the writings of Malebranche and Locke. Foremost among Hobbes's negative claims is the assertion that we have no idea of our finite spiritual substance, nor indeed of the divine spiritual substance. Hobbes writes that 'the soul is something of which we have no idea at all' and that 'we have no idea or image corresponding to the sacred name of God'.[16]

What led Hobbes to make these forthright denials? To answer this question, it will help to turn to a later work, *Leviathan*, where, in the first book 'On Man', Hobbes discusses the human mind and its faculties. What he says, here might be treated as a preface to the 'Objections' to Descartes, despite *Leviathan* being published ten years later. Hobbes argues that philosophers have been perverted in their doctrines by language. Words, he wrote, can make people 'excellently wise', but also 'excellently foolish'.[17] It is the latter effect that Hobbes observed in the writings of the scholastics. He sought to deflate their bombastic Latin by translating key terms into literal English. The imposing language is then shown to be vacuous or self-contradictory or, where it does make sense, the doctrine propounded is shown to be hopelessly far-fetched.

This literalist approach to etymology is combined with Hobbes's espousal of a strong form of concept empiricism. Early in the work, Hobbes states, in his own materialist terms, the key principle of concept empiricism – ironically, itself originally a scholastic principle – *nihil est in intellectu quod non prius fuerit in sensu*:

> There is no conception in a man's mind, which hath not at first, totally, or by parts, been begotten upon the organs of Sense.[18]

The empiricist principle is supported by the literalist understanding of Greek and Latin terms, which allows Hobbes to trace intellectual concepts back to their putative sensory roots.

Let us look at one notable example of Hobbes's approach to scholastic terminology which appears in the very first chapter of *Leviathan*. It is the Latin term *species*. Aware of the derivation from the Latin *specere*, meaning 'to look at' or 'to behold', Hobbes suggests that this term be rendered into English as 'shew, apparition, or aspect, or a being seen'. Thus, the technical scholastic phrase 'visible species' becomes, in Hobbes's English, the utterly vacuous 'visible being seen'. Hobbes then mischievously suggests that the term 'audible species' be rendered with the phrase 'audible being seen'. 'Intelligible species' becomes 'intelligible being seen' and so the satirical pattern of translation goes on. Hobbes's point is that '*species*', the central term of cognition in scholasticism, has deviated from what he calls 'natural sense' and has thus rendered the utterances of philosophers 'excellently foolish'.[19]

It is the same strategy that Hobbes then employs to undermine the intellectual and spiritual language of Cartesianism. Aware that *species* was the Latin equivalent of 'idea', his remarks about the Cartesian term follow the pattern of his deflationary view of 'species'. Hobbes, the translator of Homer and Thucydides, reminds us that the term 'idea' was 'derived from the language of the Grecians, with whom the word Εἴδω signifieth to *See*'.[20] And so an idea is literally an image, or 'that which is seen'. It is no surprise, then, that Hobbes treats ideas as sense-based pictures. Hobbes rarely uses the word 'idea' in *Leviathan*, but when he does, it means exactly this – a sensory image.[21]

In his Objections to Descartes's *Meditations*, we find Hobbes concentrating his fire on Descartes's philosophical use of the term 'idea' in connection with self-knowledge:

> As for the idea of myself, this arises from sight, if we are thinking of 'myself' as my body; and if we are thinking of the soul, then the soul is something of which we have no idea at all.[22]

For Hobbes there is no idea of a spiritual self because there is no image beyond the depictions in sense of one's own body. It is only by misusing language that Descartes can convince himself and others that there is a peculiar representation of an inner immaterial self. Thus, Hobbes locates what he takes to be a vacuity at the centre of the Cartesian system – when the mind attempts to turn away from physical things and to perceive itself, no idea and no knowledge is forthcoming. The Cartesians have been deceived by their own scholastic terminology.

When Hobbes turns to the concept of God, he again denies that there is any idea to be had.[23] The claim now, though, has a rather different significance. It is not just that we have no idea of God as a spiritual being, but that rather any attempt to conceive of his nature by finite idea must fail. God is not a corporeal being at all and, because our conceptions are limited to the pictures derived from sense, we can form no image that would begin to represent the divine nature. God's infinite being is necessarily inconceivable to finite minds like our own, and we can only characterize Him negatively (as with the negative term 'infinite' itself), or heap on Him superlatives, that express our awe, but which lack strict cognitive significance ('greatest' being one example). This allows Hobbes to interpret the biblical injunction forbidding all vain attempts to form a physical image of God as reflecting the essential incapacity of finite human thought to represent the Creator.[24]

These are the negative findings of Hobbes's examination of the Cartesian account of self-knowledge and knowledge of God. But how does Hobbes treat the self? He accepts there is a 'thinking thing' in the trivial sense of an entity that thinks, but he finds the 'thing' in question to be corporeal. When he says there is no idea of the self, what he means is that the self, when framed in characteristic Cartesian fashion as a spiritual substance perceived by the pure intellect, is a mere nothing. This self is an illusion, trading on an implicit and misleading metaphor. The only perception of ourselves that Hobbes's strict concept empiricism will allow is a perception of our physical selves by the organs of sense. This means that, for Hobbes, the sentient self is to be identified with the body – particularly its interior parts, including the heart, the brain and that section of the nervous system that is enclosed by the *pia mater*.[25]

Malebranche: 'We are but shadows to ourselves'

That Hobbes, a materialist, should reject Descartes's claim that we have an immediate idea of the spiritual self is no more than what one would expect. Surprising, though, is that Father Malebranche, who thought the soul to be 'the most noble part of our being', should also exhibit scepticism about our ability to know the nature of the soul substance. Berkeley paid close attention to what Malebranche said in this regard and Malebranche's influence on him was probably both positive and negative. One thing seems clear, though – the conclusions that Malebranche offered as to our lack of knowledge of the soul confirmed to Berkeley that something had gone seriously wrong with Descartes's account of self-knowledge in terms of ideas.

Malebranche's view of spirit is not always perfectly consistent, and even in his most important philosophical work, *Recherche de la Vérité*, we find varying pronouncements. But his most important sceptical claim, that we have no idea of our own spiritual nature, can be seen to be unchanging if we first clear up an equivocation in the term 'idea'. For Malebranche, the term can have two meanings. Loosely, it can mean 'anything that represents some object to the mind'. But Malebranche more often uses the term in the narrower, normative sense of 'anything that represents things to the mind in a way so clear that we can discover by simple perception whether such and such modifications belong to them'.[26] It is in this second sense – as a perception of the pure intellect – that Malebranche claims we lack any idea of the soul. It is this fundamental thesis that Malebranche sought to elaborate and defend.

Instead of a perspicuous representation of the soul, Malebranche held that we know ourselves by 'inner sensation' (*sentiment intérieur*) or 'consciousness'. By this he meant a murky kind of knowledge, involving confused and disconnected feelings, rather than the perceptions of pure intellect which are able to constitute a demonstrative science. These internal sensations cannot be clearly defined, and they can be known only by our direct experience of them.[27] So the modifications of the mind, familiar to us in experience, cannot become part of a fluent *scientia* in the way that the modifications of intelligible extension can constitute Euclidean geometry. Instead, we must discover the mind's properties by piecemeal empirical observation. Not only can we not deduce and predict the modifications of the mind prior to experience, but we naturally tend to mix up our sensations with perceptions of external objects, as, for example, when we see colours spread out on the surface of objects though they are really modifications of our own minds.[28]

The result is that while self-consciousness is not strictly speaking deceptive, it does not reveal what is most essential to us. Indeed, 'the consciousness we have of ourselves perhaps shows us only the least part of our being.'[29] Certainly, inner sensation proves that we exist, and Malebranche thinks this (somehow) suffices to guarantee our immortality, spirituality and freedom. But inner sensation gives no indication of what our real nature is, nor does it reveal what our soul would be like in detachment from our body.

Despite this sceptical tendency in his thought, Malebranche never doubts that, in principle, an 'idea', or perspicuous representation, of our spiritual selves is to be had. Indeed, it must be present in the mind of God, our creator, as part of the blueprint of his creation, though it remains inaccessible to finite human inquirers. Why does God deny us proper knowledge of ourselves in this way? Malebranche argues that it is for our own good. If we had a perspicuous perception of ourselves, we would no longer experience ourselves as embodied, as 'dispersed through all our members', which would be highly detrimental to the pursuit of our own well-being and to our survival in the corporeal world in which we currently find ourselves.[30]

The upshot is that, on Malebranche's view:

> We are but shadows to ourselves; to see ourselves, we must look beyond ourselves, and we shall never know what we are until we view ourselves in Him who is our light and in whom all things become light.[31]

Here Malebranche's Christian Platonism shines forth. Presupposing his normative understanding of the term 'idea', he is led to locate the idea of our own spiritual substance, along with the ideas of intelligible extension, in the mind of God. It is only by the divine light that we might one day 'view ourselves in Him', gaining thereby complete knowledge of what we are. While God has chosen to present us with the idea of extension and thus provides us with the light to understand the deductive knowledge of geometry, he has not disclosed to us an idea of the thinking subject which might ground a spiritual *scientia*. In our current state we must content ourselves with self-knowledge that is seriously defective and incomplete.

Sometimes it is said that Berkeley is close to Malebranche on the subject of self-knowledge. This was the view of A. A. Luce, who wrote in his classic study of Malebranche's influence on Berkeley:

> Berkeley regarded our self-knowledge, as Malebranche did, as partial and imperfect but immediate and quite real.[32]

Despite Malebranche's undoubted influence on Berkeley – something Luce did so much to draw our attention to – this assertion of the proximity of the two philosophers on self-knowledge cannot be sustained. Not only did Berkeley show no inclination to describe knowledge of the self as imperfect or partial, he rejected Malebranche's very ideal of self-knowledge which sought to gain a *perception* of the self. Berkeley clearly has this ideal of Malebranche's in mind when he scrawled into his Notebooks the following blunt verdict:

> Absurd that men should know the soul by idea ideas being inert, thoughtless, Hence Malbranch confuted.[33]

Berkeley's diagnosis of Malebranche's error is actually, in broad outline, no different to his diagnosis of the errors of his other contemporaries and near contemporaries. Philosophers are striving for something that cannot be had: an idea of the self. It is little wonder that in seeking this impossibility, they end up in scepticism about knowledge of the self. The cause of the scepticism is the Cartesian assumption that self-knowledge is to be treated as a form of perception, parallel to the perception of extended things. It is this assumption that has led Malebranche to pursue a chimera, and, in his disappointment, to look upon our actual knowledge of ourselves as seriously deficient. To 'confute' Malebranche we need only ponder the absurdity of his ambition of achieving an idea of the self.

Yet, Berkeley may have found something congenial in Malebranche's more general reflections on knowledge by idea. Malebranche, despite his celebration of the epistemic lucidity of ideas, also made plain their limitations. He conceded that all knowledge by idea is necessarily indirect. To know by idea is to know things 'through something different from themselves'.[34] Such knowledge is therefore inferior to a direct knowledge of things, where those things 'are intelligible by themselves'. Accordingly, Malebranche drops the language of ideas – and, indeed of representation altogether – for what he held to be the most direct form of knowledge when we grasp 'unbounded being', or God. Here there is no need for any mediating representation. In this unique case, says Malebranche, we know the being – the deity – 'through himself' (*par lui-même*).[35]

If Berkeley took something positive away from his reading of Malebranche, then it is perhaps this: knowledge need not only be had by means of idea.

Indeed, the most intimate and direct form of knowledge owes its special status to the very lack of an intervening idea. Berkeley, of course, was neither tempted by Malebranche's assertion that it is our knowledge of God that evinces this peculiar immediate relation, nor by the more general doctrine of the 'intimate union' of our minds with God's. Such a view about our relation to the divine was looked upon by Berkeley as incomprehensible and probably, also, as a form of 'enthusiasm'.[36] But Berkeley may still have noticed the *species* of knowledge that Malebranche had delineated and drawn attention to – and it may have seemed appropriate to Berkeley to apply this species of knowledge in an account of self-awareness. However, on this question of positive influence we can only speculate. What is evident in Berkeley's writings is his rejection of Malebranche's scepticism with regard to self-knowledge, and his diagnosis of this scepticism as stemming from the misguided assumption that self-knowledge should involve an idea.

Locke on the 'internal sense' of reflection

While Berkeley was no doubt struck by the doubts expressed by Hobbes and Malebranche with regard to knowledge of spiritual substance, I believe that it was Locke's subtler form of scepticism that most exercised him. Certainly, it is Locke who is the most frequent target of his critical remarks on this issue.[37] It should not be forgotten, in considering Locke's account of knowledge and reflection, that Berkeley's view of Locke would be deeply influenced – perhaps even warped – by the way in which John Toland, Anthony Collins and the Third Earl of Shaftesbury had, in different ways, sought to radicalize his philosophical legacy. Toland and Collins discovered a tendency to scepticism and materialism, while Shaftesbury extended Locke's internal sense of reflection to make sense of moral and aesthetic judgement. All three interpretations were considered by Berkeley as inimical to Christian doctrine and directly stemming from Locke's principles.

To understand the significance of Locke's view of the spiritual sphere for Berkeley we must first appreciate his overall philosophical orientation. Locke, like Hobbes but unlike Malebranche, was committed to concept empiricism. Certainly, Locke espoused a less strict concept empiricism than Hobbes, and he went further in accommodating aspects of Descartes's spiritual knowledge. But concept empiricism had the same axiomatic status in his philosophical project as it had had for Hobbes. Indeed, it is revealed in the very first sentence that Locke committed to paper on the subject of the human mind in 1671. In a manuscript he entitled 'de Intellectu humano', now known as 'Draft A' of the *Essay*, Locke began:

> I imagin that all knowleg is founded on and ultimately derives its self from sense, or something analogous to it.[38]

And after discussing sense perception itself, he tells us what he understands by 'something analogous to it':

> The other fountaine of all our knowledg though it be not sense, yet is some thing very like it & may properly enough be called sensation & is noething but the experience of the operations of our owne mindes within of which very operations being often repeated we frame certaine Ideas such as Thinkeing Beleiveing or to Thinke beleive assent doubt desire love feare hope hate &c.[39]

Here we see, in embryo, what will come to be Locke's doctrine of reflection. The perception of our own mental operations is held to be strongly analogous to sense perception, or 'sensation'. This is a view that Locke maintains throughout the three extant drafts of the *Essay*, and which he stresses and develops in the four published editions of the *Essay* that he oversaw, beginning in 1690.

In the *Essay* itself, Locke expands on this analogy between sense perception and reflection. He tells us that there are two 'Fountains of Knowledge, from whence all the *Ideas* we have, or can naturally have, do spring'. The first, which Locke calls 'sensation', is directed towards external objects, and it conveys to the mind all the ideas we have of body. The second, which Locke now calls 'reflection', is conceived on explicit analogy with sensation. It is not *literally* sensation, or sense, because it lacks a bodily organ and has 'nothing to do with external Objects'. But it parallels sense perception, as one of 'the Windows by which light is let into this *dark Room*',[40] supplying original content to the mind. Locke is happy to call it 'internal sense', and at one point even talks of 'internal sensation'.[41]

How are we to understand the parallel between sensation and reflection? Certainly, both are forms of perception for Locke. But what does this mean? After all, as we have seen, 'perception' was used by Descartes and his successors broadly to denote all kinds of cognition, including knowledge attributed to the pure intellect. Locke clearly wants to make more of the analogy than merely to indicate, in this general way, that both sense perception and reflection are forms of knowing. Locke's treatment of reflection as analogous to sense perception has, for him, the following more specific implications.

Firstly, the analogy means that we observe ourselves in a way that is familiar from the way we observe a physical object of sense. The observation of the operations of the mind may involve a peculiar 'turn', redirecting our perceptual attention inwards. But once that is accomplished, it involves the same kind of observation as the perception of external objects. We perceive our mental operations as if with an inner eye. Locke is suggesting a modest, empiricist rendering of the Cartesian inward turn:

> Mind … turns its view inward upon it self, and observes its own Actions about those *Ideas* it has, takes from thence other *Ideas*, which are as capable to be the Objects of its Contemplation as any of those it received from foreign things.[42]

Like Descartes, Locke judges that children and some adults (including even a few philosophers) have not arrived at this inward turn. So, while they are aware of the objects of sense and their 'Thoughts are immersed in Matter', they fail to notice the acts of mind that accompany these objects and therefore lack lasting ideas of reflection.[43] No doubt Hobbes was among those being chastised here.

Secondly, more narrowly, Locke bids us to recognize the passivity of the mind towards the contents of both these kinds of perceptual observation. When we observe ourselves, the ideas of our mental operations are imprinted on our minds, just as the impressions of the qualities of external bodies are passively received. The contents of reflection are beyond our power to determine or change:

> The *Understanding* can no more refuse to have, nor alter, when they are imprinted, nor blot them out, and make new ones in it self, than a mirror can refuse, alter, or obliterate the Images or *Ideas*, which, the Objects set before it, do therein produce.[44] (Emphasis in the original)

In reflection we mirror ourselves and suffer the operations of our own minds to affect our understandings, just as our senses mirror external objects in ordinary sense perception.

This perceptual model of reflection soon gives rise to an ambiguity that Locke perhaps never quite resolves. It is not clear whether the act of reflection is itself a possible object of observation, or whether it is a kind of meta-activity that is never known in the way that our other mental operations, such as believing, abstracting or doubting, are known. If we treat reflection as a mental act alongside the others, then an infinite regress will threaten with each act of reflection demanding another for us to be conscious of it, and so on *ad infinitum*. But if reflection is an unconscious meta-activity then it is not clear how it can count as a kind of perception after all. For Locke says, in more than one place, that any mental act of perceiving is conscious to us – indeed it is known by reflection.[45] One cannot help concluding that Locke's inward turn, just like Descartes's, is fraught with paradox.[46]

The situation is further complicated by Locke's characterization of consciousness itself as 'the perception of what passes in a man's own mind'.[47] It is not clear whether this is just a turn of phrase, innocent enough. If so, it would not refer to an additional perception of the mind, but would merely mark the fact that all ideas, including those reflective ones of our mental activities, are transparent to their subject. Speaking against this innocent interpretation, however, is Locke's supposition that the ideas of some of our mental operations can occur unreflectingly and perhaps unconsciously, as in a young child.[48] If this is the case, then consciousness would only be bestowed on these operations by an additional perceptual act.[49]

When Locke comes to itemize the simple ideas that are known by the internal sense of reflection there are again ambiguities. Initially he talks only of ideas of the mind's own operations, with examples such as perception, thinking, doubting, believing, reasoning, knowing, willing 'and all the different actings of our own Minds'.[50] But it becomes clear, almost immediately, that reflection will include the affective states that typically attend, or are caused by, these mental actings, for Locke tells us he is using the term 'operations' 'in a large sense'

> as comprehending not barely the Actions of the Mind about its *Ideas*, but some sort of Passions arising sometimes from them, such as is the satisfaction or uneasiness arising from any thought.[51]

The role of reflection in perceiving our affective states is confirmed later in the *Essay* when Locke tells us that 'delight and uneasiness' are ideas of sensation *and* reflection, and that passions are modes of these pleasurable and painful states.[52] At various other points in the *Essay* we are told that the ideas of power, existence, unity, duration, succession, number and life, all gain admittance to our minds by reflection as well as by sense perception.[53] Reflection thus comes to be a source of ideas that are fundamental to intellectual knowledge. When originally introduced, reflection had seemed to only explain the knowledge we have of our own actions, but in the course of the *Essay* it acquires the additional role of helping to furnish us with many of the concepts that Cartesians took to be innate. Locke held that these concepts are not ready formed in the mind *ab initio*, instead they pervade all experience, both outer and inner. The idea of an active causal power was said by Locke to be more clearly found in reflection than sensation, suggesting that this key intellectual concept was really derived from the 'internal sense'.[54]

We have, so far, expounded Locke's internal sense of reflection, but now we must relate that doctrine to his wider scepticism about the nature of spiritual substance. It is when he comes to the question of the essence of our spiritual selves that Locke makes his characteristic disavowal of knowledge. While reflection certainly reveals that something in us thinks, it does not disclose to us the inner nature of that thing.[55] Both the external senses and the inner sense of reflection only provide us with 'some few superficial Ideas of things' not with their 'internal Constitution'.[56]

As noted above, Locke wishes to clearly distinguish his position from that of Hobbes. Hobbes and the materialists deny the very existence of spiritual phenomena. They fail to recognize any kind of 'internal sense' and therefore pass over the simple ideas of our mental operations. Thus, while they acknowledge the external objects of sensation, they remain blind to the act of perception itself. This is treated by Locke as a natural human failing. In our eagerness to understand outward things, we tend to overlook the deliverances of the faculty of reflection:

> It is for want of reflection, that we are apt to think, that our Senses shew us nothing but material things. Every act of sensation, when duly considered, gives us an equal view of both parts of nature, the Corporeal and Spiritual. For whilst I know, by seeing or hearing, *etc.* that there is some Corporeal Being without me, the Object of that sensation, I do more certainly know, that there is some Spiritual Being within me, that sees and hears.[57]

But while Hobbes's straightforward materialism is eschewed, Locke does not want to commit himself to the existence of a spiritual *substance*. Notice the non-committal use of 'being' in the passage just quoted ('there is some Spiritual Being'). This statement was added to the fourth edition of the *Essay* and it seems designed both to deflect Edward Stillingfleet's charge of materialism and, yet, to fall short of endorsing a soul *substance*. Locke accepts the spiritual operations that are revealed by reflection, but, in accordance with his concept empiricism, he refrains from offering any certain claim to knowledge of the substance underlying those operations.

The passage is evidence of Locke's even-handed epistemic pessimism towards material and spiritual substance to be found in many other passages of the *Essay*. In each case our simple ideas provide us with knowledge of the existence of material and spiritual things, but they do not reveal the essence of those things, or the substances which underlie the qualities. Therefore, while we can say with certainty that these two kinds of things exist, we cannot go further and characterise their inner natures. Locke's concept empiricism precludes our intellects from having access to content not derived from sense. We are therefore in the dark not only when it comes to the nature of matter, but also with regard to the nature of spirit.

There are two ways of interpreting this even-handedness. An innocent interpretation would say that Locke wishes to caution us against preferring matter to spirit, and against assuming that the nature of matter, unlike that of spirit, is properly known to us. However, more subversive readings are available, and were alive in early reactions to the *Essay*, and it is likely that Berkeley would have favoured such readings. On one reading Locke was nodding towards a quasi-Spinozist monism.[58] By saying that the substances of both matter and spirit were unknown, he was acknowledging that they might share a hidden essence. The material and spiritual properties known to sensation and reflection, on this reading, would both inhere in a *tertium quid*. An alternative interpretation – equally subversive and perhaps carrying more weight – would treat Locke as leaving the backdoor open to a subtle, but thoroughgoing, form of materialism, according to which thinking emerges from complex combinations of material components. This suspicion gains support from Locke's 'thinking matter' hypothesis – his refusal to exclude the possibility that matter, when formed into systems 'fitly disposed', might be endowed, by God, with the faculty of thought.[59]

> We have the *Ideas* of *Matter* and *Thinking*, but possibly shall never be able to know, whether any mere material Being thinks, or no; it being impossible for us, by the contemplation of our own Ideas, without revelation, to discover, whether Omnipotency has not given to some Systems of Matter fitly disposed, a power to perceive and think, or else joined and fixed to Matter so disposed, a thinking immaterial Substance: It being, in respect of our Notions, not much more remote from our Comprehension to conceive, that GOD can, if he pleases, superadd to Matter a Faculty of Thinking.[60]

This passage continues to perplex commentators and has been the subject of extensive debate, focusing in particular on what divine 'superaddition' might mean in this context.[61] But on an interpretation that cannot be easily dismissed, Locke is allowing – at least in principle – a single naturalistic account of both bodily and spiritual powers.[62] While we can demonstrate that 'the first eternal Being cannot be Matter',[63] Locke offers no parallel proof that man is not matter. Materialism is still on the table. This is perhaps confirmed by Locke's reassurance to the reader that thinking matter leaves us no worse off from an ethical or religious point of view, and that 'all the great Ends of Morality and Religion, are well enough secure, without philosophical Proofs of the Soul's Immateriality'.[64] It also finds support in Locke's theory of personal identity which allowed a continuing subject of moral responsibility as well as the possibility of an afterlife, while suspending judgement on the question of whether there is a self-subsistent spiritual substance in man.

It is likely that Berkeley, who described the 'thinking hypothesis' as a 'dangerous opinion',[65] sensed a subversive agenda here. Through the veil of Locke's epistemic modesty and caution, Berkeley probably discerned a version of materialism receiving unvoiced endorsement. While Locke may eschew Hobbes's blanket denial of the intelligibility of the spiritual sphere, and he may dismiss the dogmatic assumption that we are acquainted with the essence of matter, he discreetly presents us with the possibility of a unified naturalism in which immaterial substances would have no place. If, like Berkeley, one thought that the simplicity and indivisibility of spiritual substance was self-evident, and, indeed, vital to morality and religion, Locke's refined, modestly stated, position would be felt as a distinct threat.

3

A notion of an active self

Berkeley was not one to spend his time trying to patch up and defend the theories of others, and his approach to self-knowledge is no exception. Berkeley questions the prevailing view, put forward by Descartes and adopted by subsequent philosophers, that the mind – if it is to be known at all – must be represented by an idea. Berkeley is not only critical of this view, he utterly rejects it. However, in developing his own distinctive position, Berkeley is willing to draw on the arguments of these thinkers. In particular, as we shall see, he sought to reconcile Descartes's view that we have immediate knowledge of an indivisible, thinking substance with the view of Descartes's critics – such as Hobbes, Malebranche and Locke – that we are in fact quite lacking in an *idea* of that substance.

In this chapter, we shall investigate what Berkeley says about how we know our own selves and our mental operations, and we shall offer an interpretation of Berkeley's term 'notion', which he comes to use – in preference to the term 'idea' – to refer to knowledge in this area.

No idea of the self

Let us start with the negative claim – one that Berkeley frequently finds an occasion to stress – that there is no *idea* of the spiritual self. As he puts it in the *Principles*,

> Our souls are not to be known in the same manner as senseless inactive objects, or by way of idea.[1]

This negative thesis was already a familiar theme in the work of Hobbes, as we saw in Chapter 2, particularly visible in his 'Objections' to Descartes's

Meditations. The denial that we have any idea of our spirit is a thesis which also overlaps with the sceptical motif in the thinking of Malebranche and Locke, although these authors allowed some representations of inner states or acts, and – for Locke in particular – these representations constituted some weak form of self-knowledge.

The originality of Berkeley lies in his treating the negative thesis as no reason for regret or philosophical despondency. For Malebranche and Locke, the lack of an idea of the soul was thought to reveal a defect in our knowledge, and to reflect our cognitive limitations. Such a defect seemed, on the face of it, undesirable, so both Malebranche and Locke went on to provide a theological justification for it. For Locke, the 'Candle, that is set up in us, shines bright enough for our purposes', and we have 'sufficient light to guide us in our conduct and to know our own maker'. Knowledge that lies beyond the cast of this light, including the nature of our own selves, is not required for our recognition of moral duty and for conduct in accordance with it.[2] While for Malebranche the confusion of the self with the body in sensation is of positive benefit to us in this life because it makes us care for our embodied self, motivating us to protect ourselves against dangers and to avoid self-neglect.[3]

Berkeley, in contrast, took the lack of an idea of the spiritual self as not a sign of our cognitive limitations at all, but rather a reflection of the very nature of the soul and of the special kind of knowledge which it called for. Philosophers had fallen into scepticism because they had not recognized that knowledge of the self involves a quite different mode of awareness than that provided by ideas.

> Surely it ought not to be looked on as a defect in a human understanding, that it does not perceive the idea of spirit, if it is manifestly impossible there should be any such *idea*.[4]

The dismissal of the search for an idea of self becomes a liberating step. In this, as in other areas, 'we have first raised a dust, and then complain, we cannot see.'[5]

This last point may again seem to bring Berkeley close to Hobbes. For Hobbes, in contrast to Malebranche and Locke, saw the search for an idea of the spiritual self as evidence of a fundamental confusion that has been foisted upon us by scholastic language, and which goes against 'natural sense'. Once we recognize the impossibility of such an idea, Hobbes thought, we can turn to our true nature, which is material. But it is precisely this materialist response to the lack of an idea of the self that Berkeley was most determined to resist. He probably has Hobbes in mind when he describes the biggest danger thrown up by the deficiencies of the perceptual model:

> This opinion [that spirits can be known by idea] may have produced a doubt in some whether they had any soul at all distinct from the body, since upon enquiry they could not find they had any idea of it.[6]

Berkeley's strategy is first to go with the negative thrust of Hobbes's critique of Descartes, denying an idea of the spiritual self, but then to show that Descartes was still right to hold that a spiritual substance is immediately knowable. It is, apparently, the Cartesian account of self-knowledge 'by manner of idea' that is causing all the trouble and engendering the scepticism of his successors. So, an alternative, non-representational, account of how we are immediately acquainted with the spiritual self must be given.

Just as the comparison with the materialist Hobbes is instructive in delineating Berkeley's position on knowledge of the spiritual self, so is a comparison with the scholastic opponent of John Locke's *Essay*, John Sergeant. Berkeley was acquainted with Sergeant's book-length critique of Locke, *Solid Philosophy Asserted, against the Fancies of the Ideists*, published in 1697.[7] Central to Sergeant's critique is a rejection of the broad use of idea that Descartes, Locke and the other 'ideists' embrace. The term 'idea', Sergeant notices, originally meant 'resemblance' or 'image', and it is abused by the 'ideists' when it is used to cover all mental objects regardless of whether they are corporeal or spiritual resemblances.

> It confounds *Corporeal* and *Spiritual* Natures, which contain the two General Objects of all our knowledges [sic]; and are, besides, *most vastly disparate*.[8]

Berkeley is as alert to this danger of the blanket use of the term 'idea' as is Sergeant in this passage, and for the same reason. Like Sergeant, he notices that 'Idea' is 'properly speaking … the picture of the Imagination'.[9] He also shares Sergeant's aversion to the sweeping use of idea for all the immediate objects of the mind because this use obscures the crucial divide between acquaintance with corporeal objects and acquaintance with our own spiritual natures. Both

Sergeant and Berkeley argue that a proper philosophical understanding of spirit will inevitably be retarded by the indiscriminate use of the term 'idea' for objects of both the outer and inner spheres.

Why can there not be an idea of the self?

Why are we not able to have an idea of the self? A particularly important section for understanding Berkeley's answer to this question is *Principles* §27. This section presents several interpretational difficulties and is to be approached with caution. It contains statements which have, I believe, been widely misread. It also contains an addition in the second edition which seems to be in tension with what has been said earlier in the section. But the opening sentences are clear enough:

> A spirit is one simple, undivided, active being: as it perceives ideas, it is called the *understanding*, and as it produces or otherwise operates about them, it is called the *will*. Hence there can be no idea formed of a soul or spirit: for all ideas whatever, being passive and inert ... they cannot represent unto us, by way of image or likeness, that which acts. (Emphasis in the original)

The reason why we cannot have an idea of a spirit is because of the utter heterogeneity of ideas and spirits. There is no resemblance between them. Ideas are passive; spirit is active. Ideas are causally inefficacious and inert; spirits initiate change. As Berkeley puts it later in the *Principles*, mind is 'more distant and heterogenous' from ideas 'than light is from darkness'.[10]

We shall say more about the active–inert contrast in a moment. First, though, I would like to point to the other fundamental difference between spirits and ideas in the passage just quoted: spirits are 'simple' and 'undivided', while ideas are not. By the time of the *Principles* Berkeley has come to reject the simple ideas of Locke's system as non-existent abstractions, and so now nothing in the realm of ideas has the simplicity and indivisibility required to represent the soul.[11] It is unclear whether *minima sensibilia* still survive in Berkeley's thinking at the time of the *Principles*, although they were often referred to in the Notebooks and were also evident in the *Essay on Vision*.[12] But *minima* are, at the best of times, peculiar objects of perception. It is surely wrong to think of them along the lines of pixels on a computer screen, or the tiny coloured stones that make up a mosaic. Sensible *minima* are rather dimensionless vanishing points, bearing comparison with both physical indivisibles (atoms) and mathematical points. Like atoms, they are somehow able to clump together to form extended objects of perception; unlike atoms they lack even notional parts and thus amount to extensionless points.[13] So *minima* lack any unambiguous and positive simplicity.

The simplicity of the soul, and its role in distinguishing the mind from the objects of sense and thought, is an important theme which we shall return to. It marks a significant difference between Berkeley and others who denied we have an idea of the soul. Neither Hobbes nor Locke, for example, insisted on the indivisibility of the thinking self.[14] On spiritual indivisibility Berkeley is resolutely Cartesian, although the most direct influence may actually be Socrates's defence of the immortality of the soul in Plato's *Phaedo*, a dialogue which we know had an early impact on his thought and which he looked upon as a special authority throughout his career.[15]

We will look more closely at the question of simplicity in Chapter 8, but now let us return to the question of what Berkeley means when he says that spirit is active, but ideas are not. It would clearly not be enough to treat activity here as motion, change or flow.[16] That would be to seriously misinterpret Berkeley's sense of the passive, for he frequently states that we perceive *movement* by idea, and he often stresses that movement itself is, in this sense, passive and inert. Activity is clearly meant to indicate the causal origin of movement or change. Ideas are inactive because 'there is nothing of power or agency included in them'.[17]

Can we not see the causal power of a flood as it breaks down fences and walls, uprooting trees? Is this not to perceive the active power in our perceptual ideas of a torrent of water? Berkeley thinks not. Indeed, he thinks it is obvious that we should reply in the negative, because 'to be satisfied of the truth of this, there is nothing else requisite but a bare observation of our ideas'.[18] What he is getting at is the lack of *original* causal power in objects that we witness as we observe the moving water and the changes that appear in its wake. Berkeley's attention is focused on what he calls 'production'. He writes, 'one idea or object of thought cannot *produce*, or make any alteration in another'.[19] I think we should take him as agreeing with Malebranche – and with Hume after him – that although we may perceive a law-like regularity when observing nature, the productive power behind this regularity is nowhere to be seen. Perception discovers only the repeated concatenation of events.

> That food nourishes, sleep refreshes, and fire warms us; that to sow in the seed-time is the way to reap in the harvest, and, in general, that to obtain such or such ends, such or such means are conducive, all this we know, not by discovering any necessary connexion between our ideas, but only by the observation of the settled Laws of Nature.[20]

Because we assume that perception by idea is the only kind of knowledge, our desire to know real causation leads us to go 'wandering after second causes'. In other words, we take ideas, which are only signs or 'second' causes, as the first, productive causes. The moving water is really a sign. A sign that we, with our experience of liquids, have learnt to read. Thus, we can predict that objects standing in the way of the torrent will be swept away, and we attribute to the perception of water this causal power, when in fact it is only a sign of what is to come.

> For when we perceive certain ideas of sense constantly followed by other ideas, and we know this is not of our doing, we forthwith attribute power and agency to the ideas themselves, and make one the cause of another, than which nothing can be more absurd and unintelligible.[21]

The perception of ideas only ever reaches as far as effects. We may detect and comprehend constant laws that govern these effects, which we can then exploit to survive and prosper. But these are causes in name only. They grant us foresight but not insight. They do not reveal *how* causation works and *how* the effects are produced. Such knowledge of causation is directly revealed to us only in our own mental power of will. It is the power of our minds, governing the production of ideas in our imagination and initiating the movement of our limbs, that is the source of our knowledge of the active power of causation. Here we know causation from within.[22]

A relative notion of the self?

The active, simple spiritual self eludes any kind of representation by idea. That much is clear. But it may now seem, in the light of how Berkeley goes on in the section in question, *Principles* §27, that Berkeley allows only an indirect route to self-knowledge. For some interpreters, Berkeley's view is that we have a merely *relative*, understanding of the spirit.

> Such is the nature of *spirit* or that which acts, that it cannot be of itself perceived, but only by the effect which it produceth.[23]

It is this sentence, I think, that is responsible for leading some readers of Berkeley's philosophy of spirit right off track. There is a tendency to treat the claim that spirit 'cannot be of itself perceived' as equivalent to spirit 'cannot be of itself known'. It has therefore been thought that Berkeley thinks the nature of spirit can be known only indirectly, never 'of itself'. We cannot encounter active spirit immediately, but only by way of the effects (ideas) that it produces. We see the smoke, but never the fire that produces it.

Here we confront not just a minor misreading, but a failure to grasp the very aim of Berkeley's philosophy of spirit. On this 'relative notion' interpretation, his philosophy is played out in the framework of ideas – spirit is essentially mysterious, only to be known in an indirect or relative way as that which causes, or produces, the ideas in question. This is in danger of attributing to Berkeley's treatment of spirit the kind of philosophical scepticism about the 'inward essence and constitution of things' that he had found in Locke's *Essay* and which he had found so unacceptable.[24]

George Pitcher was the originator of the relative notion interpretation, arguing that 'we have a merely relative notion of spirit'.[25] Daniel Flage, who has been the most sophisticated proponent of this view, reminds us that the term 'to perceive' often meant 'to know' in the early modern period, and that Berkeley sometimes uses 'know' and 'perceive' interchangeably when discussing ideas.[26] Accordingly, when Berkeley says spirit 'cannot be of itself be perceived', Flage has taken him to be saying that spirit cannot be of itself *known*, but that it can only be picked out indirectly through its relation to ideas.[27] Flage has written that in Berkeley's view 'one does not know what a mind is in itself', all that one can do is 'single out a mind as that which thinks, wills and perceives, where thinking, willing and perceiving are taken to be either relations between minds and ideas or properties of the mind'.[28]

The interpretation that I am presenting is in fundamental opposition to 'the relative notion' of spirit advanced by Pitcher and Flage. I wish to show that, on the contrary, spirit can indeed 'be of itself known' in Berkeley's philosophy. Perception is, after all, only one species of knowledge. In ruling out direct *perception* of spirit by idea, Berkeley is not ruling out direct *knowledge* of the nature of spirit. Flage may be right that Berkeley speaks of knowing and perceiving interchangeably in contexts where he is discussing knowledge by idea. But the fact that ideas are indeed a kind of immediate knowledge does not mean they are the only kind of immediate knowledge. Berkeley tells us quite clearly that there is direct inner knowledge that does not take the form of perception or idea. In the *Three Dialogues*, Philonous cautions Hylas against treating knowledge of the self as perception:

> I know what I mean by the terms I and myself; and I know this immediately, or intuitively, though I do not perceive it as I perceive a triangle, a colour, or a sound.[29]

The relative notion interpretation leaves us no way of understanding this immediate non-perceptual acquaintance with the nature of our own self that is so clearly asserted by Berkeley in this sentence, and in the passage of which it is part.[30] The self, on Pitcher's and Flage's interpretation, becomes a kind of black box – an 'x' – the inscrutable thing that actively produces diverse ideas in my consciousness.[31]

In contrast to the relative notion interpretation, I submit that we can only understand *Principles* §27, and bring it into harmony with Berkeley's assertion of 'immediate and intuitive' self-knowledge, if we appreciate that here Berkeley is making a negative point, delineating the limits of perceptual knowledge. It is a variation on the theme: 'I do not perceive [spirit] as I perceive a triangle, a colour, or a sound.' The perceptual species of knowledge, he is saying, fails to reveal anything more than an indirect determination of what spirit is. If we treat this statement of Berkeley's as a *positive* claim about what self-knowledge consists in then, I believe, his philosophy of spirit will be quite impenetrable to us.

Two species of immediate knowledge

'Human knowledge', writes Berkeley, 'may naturally be reduced to two heads, that of ideas, and that of spirits'.[32] Knowledge is, on Berkeley's account, a genus

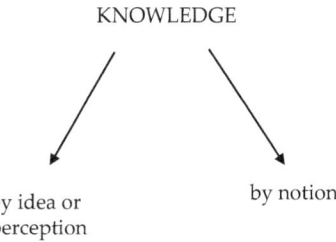

Figure 3.1 Two species of direct knowledge.

that is made up of two species. Perceptual knowledge by idea, discussed in *Principles* §27, is only one species of knowledge. The other species is knowledge of spirit and its acts which are known directly, but not by idea. It is this second species of knowledge which Berkeley comes to refer to, from 1734 onwards, as knowledge by notion.

Now these two diverse forms of immediate knowledge will go on to be the basis for other kinds of *indirect* knowledge. The immediate perception of an idea, when supplemented by 'suggestion', or inference, may allow us to indirectly perceive further ideas, as, for example, when we hear the sound of a coach and indirectly perceive the vehicle by the suggestion of visual and tactile ideas.[33] Or when I see your face turn pale or pink and I indirectly infer your fright or embarrassment.[34]

But let us put aside these indirect forms of knowledge and let us concentrate here on the second species of direct knowledge, knowledge by notion. It would be wrong to treat knowledge by notion as just a minor exception to a general commitment to the 'new way of ideas' (Stillingfleet) or 'ideism' (Sergeant) on Berkeley's part. After all, knowledge by notion constitutes our grasp of our own spiritual selves, and of spiritual substance. It also furnishes us with the concept of active power and, thus, of causation in general. Our concepts of substance and cause are not derived from sensory ideas of corporeal things, but are founded instead on the immediate awareness we have of our active, spiritual *being*. Self, causation, substance are the central pillars of Berkeley's spirit-based ontology, so this species of knowledge is no footnote or afterthought.

Knowledge by notion is also the source of further intellectual and metaphysical concepts. In our immediate and intuitive acquaintance with our self we find a pathway not only to the concepts of substance and causation, but also to simplicity, unity and number, as well as the basic concepts of moral and aesthetic judgement. Indeed, Berkeley's doctrine of notions expands as a growing range of objects of knowledge come to be included in it after the first edition of the *Principles*. Most notably, in the Middle Period, after his return journey across the Atlantic, Berkeley adds *relations* to his list of knowledge by notions. And in the last phase of his development he explicitly extends his doctrine of notions to include the relations of 'likeness' and 'parity', without which any conceptual thought would surely be unthinkable.[35]

I shall explore the expanding doctrine of notions in later chapters, where I will make the case for treating the doctrine of notions as a rationalist element in Berkeley's thought, which has some measure of affinity to early modern innatism, and which Berkeley ultimately identifies with a dynamic understanding of Plato's Forms. For the time being, I wish to address the question of what knowledge by notion involves, if not ideas.

Knowing through doing

The notions of the self and its acts do not, in Berkeley's view, amount to beholding ourselves in a Cartesian inner-theatre. We do not know our activities as an intellectual spectacle, but through our mentally performing them. Notions signify the transparent and immediate knowledge that the doer has of her doing. To exercise the mind's operations is to know those operations from within.[36] Kenneth Winkler makes this elemental point in the following way:

> The acts and operations of the mind are not known insofar as we contemplate and view them; they are known insofar as we enact and perform them. The mind itself is also not an object that we contemplate and view, but a thing known through acting, operating, or performing.[37]

Now, these are the words of Kenneth Winkler, not of George Berkeley. One might wonder why Berkeley does not say something like this himself if it successfully describes the special way in which, according to him, we know our own mental activity and the mind itself. The answer is, I believe, that Berkeley recognizes no other possible understanding of notions. It is enough to describe the knowledge in question as 'immediate': that is, unmediated.[38]

He has not countenanced the possibility that a reader might treat notions as things that stand between the acts and the mind, since this would so obviously be to claim that the knowledge was not immediate at all. Winkler is really correcting a misapprehension amongst readers of Berkeley, who would treat notions as objects separate from the operations they give knowledge of.[39] Notions are not items or entities, or even representations. Rather, they are the epistemological transparency of the active mind to itself, a transparency that is not susceptible to the division between a knower and an object of knowledge.

Once we have overcome the tendency to reify notions as peculiar things, meanings, concepts or representations that mediate our knowledge of the inner, then there may be little more to be said than this: my own mental acting is known through itself, or – to repeat Winkler's flourish of synonyms – 'through acting, operating, or performing'.[40]

Fichte's discussion of 'intellectual intuition' (*Intellektuelle Anschauung*) makes a useful point of comparison:

> Intellectual intuition is the immediate consciousness that I act and of what I do when I act. It is because of this that it is possible for me to know something because I do it. That we possess such a power of intellectual intuition is not something that can be demonstrated by means of concepts, nor can an understanding of what intellectual intuition is be produced from concepts. This is something everyone has to discover immediately within himself; otherwise, he will never become acquainted with it at all.[41]

Berkeley's account of immediate self-knowledge through the exercise of our mental powers has notable advantages. Like Fichte's intellectual intuition, it escapes problems in Descartes's own perceptual account of self-knowledge that we mentioned in Chapter 2. One problem, initially remarked on by Hobbes, was of an infinite regress that threatened to arise from self-knowledge by idea, as each act demanded a further idea of itself, and so on *ad infinitum*. This regress can only begin where there is a perception of the mind's own states and actions, and therefore it does not affect Berkeley's account. We also mentioned further problems connected with ideas of mental activity such as willing and undergoing passions. In particular, the perceptual model has trouble accounting for our ownership of our volitions – it seems to make us mere onlookers, peering at our acts of will rather than being their moving force. This problem also disappears in Berkeley's account of self-knowledge.

For Berkeley there is neither a need to engage in further acts of self-perception, nor is it necessary to represent the self in some other way. Being active is enough. When willing the movement of my arm, I am the cause that knows itself. To suggest that I need an *idea* of my willing in addition to the mental action is to needlessly multiply mental contents, leading to paradox and scepticism. In dropping the perceptual account, Berkeley makes self-knowledge indubitable and intuitive. We know ourselves not 'through something different from ourselves', as Malebranche characterizes knowledge by idea,[42] rather we know ourselves *through ourselves*.

Berkeley thus distinguishes between two different, but equally essential, elements in conscious experience: on the one hand there are ideas, the inert perceptual objects that are employed in our mental actions; and on the other hand there are those actions themselves which are known through themselves, *per se nota*. Berkeley thinks that the mistake of his fellow philosophers has been their failure to distinguish between these two quite different kinds of awareness by using the term 'idea' indiscriminately to cover both. This terminological laxity has meant that Berkeley's contemporaries have lost sight of the distinctive non-perceptual awareness that comes with spiritual action. This, in turn, is the source of scepticism about the spiritual self, expressed in different ways by Hobbes, Malebranche and Locke. These philosophers have all been led, by their attachment to the perceptual paradigm, to engage in the quixotic quest for a *perception* of the active self, analogous to the perceptions we have of corporeal things.

The 'grand Mistake'

Berkeley held that our tendency to treat self-knowledge as mediated by ideas results from our fascination with the corporeal things of sense perception. This fixation on the things of outward perception means that we unwittingly bring to the inner sphere the wholly incongruous language of sensory perception. The inner is thus modelled on the outer. In the Notebooks, Berkeley makes the following remark:

Speech metaphorical more than we imagine. Insensible things & their modes, circumstances &c exprest for [the] most part by words borrow'd from things sensible. The reason's plain. Hence manyfold Mistakes.[43]

The reference to 'insensible things and their modes' does not, of course, denote material things too minute to detect by sense, but spiritual beings and their modes of operation. These are 'insensible' because they cannot, even in principle, be perceived by the senses. These spiritual beings, he says, have been unthinkingly described using the metaphor of sense. The 'manyfold Mistakes' are the result of our taking this metaphorical language quite literally. This confusion, Berkeley held, lies at the root of the application of the language of ideas to the active mind and its operations, as is confirmed by a remark later appended to the entry we have just quoted:

> The grand Mistake is that we think we have Ideas of the Operations of our Minds. Certainly this Metaphorical dress is an argument we have not.[44]

'Idea' is, as we have seen, used by Berkeley to refer to the objects of sense experience, and their representation in memory and imagination. 'The grand Mistake' is to use 'idea' *metaphorically* when speaking of the operations of spirit. 'A philosopher should abstain from metaphor,' as Berkeley later tells us.[45] The particular metaphor in question blinds us to the distinctiveness of spiritual knowledge. The power of the sensory thus has a tendency to infect our very understanding of ourselves and to leave us unable to comprehend our own spiritual nature.

It is this 'grand Mistake' that Berkeley returns to in the *Principles* when he observes that

> nothing seems more to have contributed towards engaging men in controversies and mistakes, with regard to the nature and operations of the mind, than the being used to speak of those things, in terms borrowed from sensible ideas.[46]

The 'grand Mistake' is really another way of characterizing the essential error of treating self-knowledge as mediated by perception. As we have seen an idea is, as Descartes defined it, 'whatever is immediately perceived by the mind'.[47] Its original meaning, as Descartes recognized and Hobbes stressed in his Objections to Descartes, is an appearance, or even picture, of sense.

While the philosophical use of the term 'idea' certainly aims at a more abstract sense, it does not escape the perceptual metaphor. At some level it affirms an analogy between sense perception of an external object and the putative inner perception of the self and its acts. This analogy is fatal in Berkeley's view. It blinds us to the most fundamental ontological and epistemological division that we are calling 'Berkeley's dualism' – the division between 'active, indivisible substances' and 'inert, fleeting, dependent beings'.[48]

Hume and the grand mistake

Berkeley seems not to have read Hume's *Treatise on Human Nature*, the three books of which were published during 1739–40, five years or so before *Siris*. But we can construct a response, on Berkeley's behalf, to Hume's sceptical reflections on spiritual substance that were presented in the First Book of the *Treatise*.[49] Hume famously observed that when he 'enters most intimately into what I call *myself*', he 'always stumble[s] on some particular perception or other, of heat or cold, light or shade, love or hatred, pain or pleasure'.[50] On registering this introspective failure to encounter his own mind or spirit as a simple and enduring entity, Hume proceeds to analyse the mind as nothing more than a 'bundle or collection of different perceptions',[51] and to explain his previous conviction that the self is simple and continuous as a mistaken or fictional belief engendered by the 'smooth passage of the imagination from one mental state to the next'.[52]

The striking feature of Hume's self-examination is that it amounts to nothing more than a search for perceptions. True, 'perception' may be meant in the widest sense, comprising the process of 'perceiving' rather than just the result of such a process.[53] What is not in doubt, however, is that Hume is wedded to the perceptual model of knowledge quite as much as any of his contemporaries and early modern predecessors. In this – if not in much else – he is blithely Cartesian. He is happy to use the term 'perception' to cover all the possible contents of thought and experience, and thus for all the immediate objects of knowledge. Knowledge is only by way of perception and Hume allows no alternative mode of knowledge which might answer to Berkeley's 'notions'.

'Perceptions', in Hume's terminology, actually comprise two classes of mental content, 'impressions' and 'ideas', which are distinguished by the greater vivacity of the former. Impressions are also found to temporally precede their corresponding ideas. Hume treats the doctrine of self-awareness that he opposes, and which he finds endorsed by 'some metaphysicians' – among whom Berkeley presumably belongs – as the (unlikely) claim that the philosopher may have an impression, or vivid perception, of the self. The metaphysician can 'perceive something simple and continu'd, which he calls *himself*'.[54] Hume never entertains the possibility that what is simple and continued may not be known by perceptions at all, but rather through its 'acting, operating, or performing' with, or on, perceptions. He thus fails to address the views of the metaphysician we are discussing. This may be a result not so much of Hume's failure to read the relevant passages in Berkeley, but rather of his tendency to read them through the lens of his own perceptual model of knowledge. The doctrine of notions seems to have passed him by.

Hume's bundle conception of the self would no doubt be diagnosed by Berkeley as vividly symptomatic of the 'grand Mistake' of speaking of spiritual beings and their operations using the 'metaphorical dress' of sense. This diagnosis would be supported by Hume's comparison of the mind to 'a kind of theatre', where 'several perceptions successively make their appearance; pass, re-pass, glide away, and mingle in an infinite variety of postures and situations'. Hume is cautious with this analogy and explicitly disowns the spatial and material connotations of talking of a theatre, but he seems untroubled by the implication that the mind has become a mere spectacle, the object of perception. Nor does Hume seem to notice that the analogy implicitly presupposes, but utterly fails to encompass, the perceiver itself.

It is well-known that Berkeley himself went through a quasi-Humean phase in his Notebooks, and he was even led to make the assertions that the 'Mind is a congeries of Perceptions' and that 'the very existence of Ideas constitutes the soul.'[55] At this moment in his development he held, like Hume, that no mental contents apart from particular perceptions are uncovered by introspection.[56]

> Consult, ransack your Understanding what find you there besides several perceptions or thoughts?[57]

However, we soon find Berkeley raising a doubt about this proto-Humean position.

> The Understanding seemeth not to differ from its perceptions or Ideas. Qu. What must one think of the Will & passions.[58]

Not long after these doubts have hardened into the assertion that volitions are 'no ideas',[59] and that even 'to ask have we an idea of the Will or volition is nonsense', for 'an idea can resemble nothing but an idea.'[60] Berkeley now arrives at the ontological and epistemological dualism which constitutes his great departure from the 'new way of ideas', and soon we find him noting that 'the will and the Understanding may very well be thought two distinct beings'.[61] It is at this point that he begins to use the locution 'grand Mistake' for those who, ignoring this division, seek to treat our knowledge of spirit and its activities as mediated by ideas.[62] It is most likely also around this time that he returns to the earlier entry 176, inscribing on the verso page of his Notebook the forthright statement: 'The grand Mistake is that we think we have Ideas of the Operations of our Minds.'[63] This mistake is now something that Berkeley has recognized, and Hobbes is charged with making it,[64] and there can be no doubt that Hume would have been charged with making it too.

Self-forgetting and the Master Argument

It may seem that Berkeley's doctrine of notions is not a theory of self-reflection at all. After all, it seems to rule out any special episode of reflection. When we are mentally active, we enjoy that activity and know it transparently – so why should a further faculty of reflection be required? Yet, Berkeley continues to use the term 'reflection' in this regard,[65] and although reflection is neither conceived along Lockean lines as an internal sense, nor as a Cartesian perception of the intellect turning towards itself, Berkeley must be giving the term *some* significance. How are we to make sense of an act of reflection in the framework of Berkeley's philosophy of spirit?

A clue is provided by the Master Argument. Now, I do not wish to judge the soundness of the Master Argument here – a question that belongs to an assessment of his immaterialism, rather than to a discussion of his philosophy of spirit – but I do wish to ask what the Master Argument tells us about Berkeley's view of self-awareness. Berkeley offers the sceptical reader a famous deal. He will rest his whole case for immaterialism upon the outcome of a single challenge.

> If you can but conceive it possible for one extended moveable substance, or in general, for any one idea or anything like an idea, to exist otherwise than in a mind perceiving it, I shall readily give up the cause: and as for all that *compages* of external bodies which you contend for, I shall grant you its existence.[66]

Why is Berkeley confident that the result of this challenge will go his way? It is because he thinks the reader will be so immersed in ideas as to forget the perceiving and acting mind upon which those ideas are dependent.

> When we do our utmost to conceive the existence of external bodies, we are all the while only contemplating our own ideas. But the mind taking no notice of itself, is deluded to think it can and doth conceive bodies existing unthought of or without the mind.

And Berkeley thinks that 'a little attention will discover to anyone the truth and evidence of what is here said'.

The Master Argument, as I understand it, invokes a process of self-awareness, in which attention is withdrawn from mental accusatives, or ideas, and fixed instead on the mind's enjoyment[67] of its own *operations*. The argument trades on making self-evident what is passed over when we are occupied by the *objects* of our mental operations, or ideas. In those moments of absorption in ideas, 'the mind takes no notice of itself'. It is on these occasions that it becomes possible to believe in the existence of those ideas in complete independence of mind. Berkeley thinks that it is enough to remind ourselves of the mental operations we are continually enjoying as we try to imagine things existing without the mind. We may then comprehend what he treats as the self-defeating task of entertaining ideas in the absence of an active spirit.

So, whatever the final persuasiveness of the Master Argument, Berkeley takes our active mental life to be characterised by two different kinds of consciousness – perception or contemplation of ideas and enjoyment of mental operations. The contemplation can, in certain everyday episodes, monopolize our attention. When we attend less to this contemplation, and more to the mental activity that is inseparable from these ideas, we may be said to be reflective. Reflexion is not a perceptual act, but rather attention to one aspect of our experience – enjoyment of our mental activities – which is always ongoing and available to awareness.[68]

The role of language in the notion of spirit

In interpreting self-awareness by notion, I have so far said nothing about language. Yet Berkeley's makes quite frequent references to linguistic meaning in discussing notions and self-knowledge. He repeatedly makes the point that certain words – like 'myself', spirit and the different words for mental operations – possess (linguistic) meaning in spite of there being no idea before the mind when we utter them. Section 27 of the *Principles*, about which we have had much to say in this chapter, ends as follows in the 1734 edition:

> It must be owned ... that we have some notion of soul, spirit, and the operations of the mind, such as willing, loving, hating, in as much as we know or understand the meaning of those words.[69]

Why does Berkeley think that reminding us of our understanding the meaning of the words is so important? One may be tempted to see Berkeley as advancing a reductive theory of the notion of 'I' in terms of linguistic competence. On this view, Berkeley would be making a quasi-Wittgensteinian move, treating the semantic content of first-person terms as to be exhaustively explicated by their use in our language games. The words would thus have a meaning that is not derived from any inner experience that they denote, but from the rule-governed use that is made of them in the public sphere of communication.[70]

But such a view would misconstrue Berkeley's intentions. He makes reference to the meaning of these terms in an evidential way. He does not claim that the relevant linguistic use constitutes their meaning; rather he claims the fact we find these terms meaningful is prima facie evidence that they indeed have reference and are not just 'blind windows'. As Kenneth Pearce has argued, the words used for spirits and their actions are 'genuine referring expressions', or as A. D. Woozley asserted 'it is clear that "my mind" does denote, that each of us, in the case of his own mind, has privileged acquaintance with what it denotes'.[71] When Berkeley points to the indisputable fact that we use these terms with meaning, despite our not having ideas that correspond to them, he wishes to bring to our attention our direct acquaintance with the mind and its actions.

Now, in putting forward such a position, Berkeley is departing from the Lockean view of semantics, at least as it is traditionally understood. Locke's approach to meaning, as it is initially articulated in the opening chapters of Book Three of the *Essay*, appears to make ideas essential to the meaningfulness of words:

> The use then of Words, is to be the sensible Marks of *Ideas*; and the *Ideas* they stand for, are their proper and immediate signification.[72]

Locke, however, qualifies this simple view later in Book Three in a way that drew the interest of Berkeley. In his discussion of 'particles', in Chapter 7, Locke allows that while most words are meaningful by virtue of their referring to ideas, there are a significant few that 'shew or intimate some particular action' of the mind 'relating to those *Ideas*'.[73] Locke's comments about particles are brief but suggestive, and Berkeley took note. In the Notebooks there is a series of entries, 661–7,[74] that express a reaction to Locke's view of particles. In the final entry of this series, 667, Berkeley sums up what he sees as the true import of Locke's concession about particles:

> Tis allow'd that Particles stand not for Ideas & yet they are not said to be empty useless sounds. The truth on't is they stand for the operations of the mind i.e. volitions.

Berkeley has caught Locke allowing that we can speak of our mental acts without the mediation of ideas. Berkeley takes this as an indication that Locke would be able to recognize the more general truth that words referring to the self and its actions are not 'empty useless sounds', despite their having no idea attached to them, but that they 'stand for the operations of the mind'.

One will notice that this last quoted phrase shows that Berkeley has silently modified Locke's view in this entry in the Notebooks. He has Locke treating particles like nouns 'standing for' the operations of the mind, while Locke himself had said – in a quasi-emotivist vein – that they 'shew or intimate the actions of the Mind'. This move is, of course, connected with Berkeley's own view that the terms in question are genuine referring expressions. But whatever the accuracy of the reading of this chapter of the *Essay*, these entries in the Notebooks taken together confirm that Berkeley took Locke to have recognized, *malgré lui*, that we may be acquainted with the actions of our spirits in the absence of an idea of them.

Perhaps this sheds light on another entry in the Notebooks, coming very soon after, in which Berkeley passes judgement on the value of the different Books of Locke's *Essay*:

> Locke's great oversight seems to be that he did not Begin with his Third Book at least that he had not some thought of it at first. Certainly the 2 1st books don't agree with what he says in the 3 d.[75]

My suggestion, which I will develop in the next chapter, is that Berkeley is reflecting on the potential of the chapter on particles, which has just been remarked on, to undermine Locke's well-known official empiricist philosophy in the first two Books of the *Essay*. For if Locke allowed that we can meaningfully talk about the self and its acts without having ideas of them before our minds, then he would seem to cast doubt on his treatment of reflexion as an internal sense in Book Two. This would also, as we shall see in due course, imply a relaxation of the implacable opposition to innate notions that Locke voiced in Book One. It is this same recognition implied in Locke's treatment of particles that, I submit, Berkeley hopes to awaken in the reader of his *Principles* when he says that whatever dogmas we may hold about semantics, we must recognize that, though we have no idea of the mind and its activities, our language about the self still has meaning.

In this chapter, we have seen how Berkeley's view of what he comes to call the 'notions' of the self and its operations indicates that the mind has intuitive access to its active nature, unmediated by any imagery or by any kind of abstract intellectual representation. Instead, we know ourselves immediately through performing our mental activity. Inner experience is richer than the 'new way of ideas' allows. While we have many varied ideas, we also have immediate awareness of our own causal power to produce and direct those ideas in our mental operations.

4

Notions and innatism

We have seen how self-knowledge, for Berkeley, involves no idea or perception of the mind, but a transparent knowledge through doing. He began to systematically refer to this transparent knowledge with the term 'notion' in the Middle Period, when, in 1734, he prepared new editions of the *Principles* and *Three Dialogues*. In this chapter, I wish to examine what we might characterize as the 'rationalist' significance of notions and their relation to early modern innatism. Ultimately, I will not recommend that we classify the doctrine of notions as 'innatist', but I do believe the affinity with innatism is striking and it allows us to understand Berkeley's fundamental dissatisfaction with the philosophy of his empiricist predecessors, particularly Locke.

Berkeley's notions constitute an expanding doctrine that comes to greater prominence in his thought with time. In the Heroic Period, one's own mind is said to be known directly without the representation of an idea, as are causality and substance. He also indicates that the emotions (but not sensations of pain and pleasure) and moral qualities, such as virtue and goodness, are to be known in this peculiar way, and he at least implies that unity is too. Berkeley then extends the list of different things that notions give us a knowledge of, significantly adding *relations* in 1734,[1] and adding *sameness* or *equality* ('parity') and *beauty* in Siris of 1744.[2] In the Middle Period and the Final Period, the wider rationalist import of notions is also made more explicit. Indeed, as we shall see, the very term 'notion' that he introduces is strongly suggestive of a non-empiricist element in his thinking. This element is most visible in *Siris*. I have represented the expansion of the doctrine of notions in the three main periods of Berkeley's development in the appendix, Table 1.

Notions and *notiones*

The term 'notion' is one with a rich historical background in philosophy. This history will be easily overlooked if we rely on our own intuitions about the contemporary English word 'notion', which can often mean just a vague idea ('she may have some notion of what is being said', 'he hasn't got the faintest notion', etc.).

We might begin by noting that the Latin *notio* (plural *notiones*) had a rather narrow use prior to Berkeley. This noun was derived from the verb *noscere*, to know, and had been used in philosophical contexts to signify a special kind of inner cognition. In St. Augustine's writings, the term referred to an intimate spiritual knowledge that 'we have received through no gateway of the flesh'.[3] Augustine's notions were not pictures or images rooted in bodily sensation, and the term *notiones* was used in conscious distinction to *imagines*. Notions for Augustine covered emotions and acts of will which were known by a kind of direct, internal insight.[4] Indeed, for Augustine, passions are not sensual perceptions, but 'have their source in the soul itself' (as Susan James puts it) 'and are essentially acts of will'.[5] As such they are known by notions.

In the Cartesian tradition, notions (Latin *notiones*; French *notions*) were transparently known intellectual objects – the elements of rational thought.[6] Descartes links the meaning of the word to its etymology: *notiones* are the simplest constituents of knowledge that are *per se nota* – 'known through themselves', or 'self-evident' as the phrase is rendered in the now standard English translation.[7] He distinguished notions which were 'simple' or 'primary' (*primæ notiones*) from those which were 'common' (*notiones communes*). Primary notions are the simple components of intellectual thought (*ex quibus cogitationes nostræ componuntur*) that are known by the pure intellect. Common notions, on the other hand, are propositional in form and are the principles of reasoning, such as the rational truths that ground Euclidean geometry and other purely rational sciences, including metaphysics. Among these are, for example, 'the whole is greater than the parts' and 'nothing comes from nothing'. Both primary and common notions had, for Descartes, an innate origin.

We might also notice that the term 'notion' was Locke's preferred term for the innate mental content that he sought to deny. The non-imagistic character of innate concepts is, no doubt, the reason that Locke entitled the First Book of his *Essay* 'Of Innate Notions',[8] and why in the course of that book he targets what he describes not only as 'innate Notions', but also 'primary Notions', 'Notions naturally imprinted', 'original Notions', 'common Notions', and so on.[9] We should not forget that the phrase 'innate ideas', a commonplace in the contemporary secondary literature on Locke, is one he himself used hardly at all.

As we have already seen, Berkeley makes reference to the pure intellect when discussing the objects of spiritual knowledge in his early philosophy,[10] and by choosing the term 'notion' he is no doubt conscious of the Cartesian usage, just as Descartes probably had one eye on Augustine. Berkeley, too, treated notions as knowledge that is perspicuous to our minds, and which is not derived from the objects of sensory perception, or from any source external to the mind. By notions we have an immediate and intuitive understanding that involves no picturing nor any use of imagery, a point on which Augustine and Descartes concurred. So, it is not surprising, given the history of the term, that Berkeley uses 'notion' to express a fundamental contrast with 'ideas' which, in his understanding, are the images of sense and are therefore equivalent to *imagines*.

Berkeley's strange reticence about innatism

It is a remarkable fact deserving of wider recognition that Berkeley never published a word in favour of Locke's polemic against innatism. In the early Heroic Period, he remained silent on the issue: while in his middle and final periods – particularly in *Siris*, but also in his sermons and, by implication at least, in *Alciphron* – he tends to put innatism in a positive light and even dismisses Locke's critique for targeting a man of straw.[11]

Now, the reason for the lack of direct reference to Locke's attack on innatism in Berkeley's earlier published works is not immediately clear. Some have taken it as a sign that Berkeley thought Locke was perfectly right and the issue was now closed. This is the view of J. O. Urmson who writes 'since Locke had repudiated any such [innatist] view, Berkeley did not think it necessary to argue against it'.[12] But this is a bold and potentially hazardous interpretational step. Berkeley may have had a variety of reasons for being reticent about this question. It may be that Berkeley had little sympathy for the thrust of Locke's attack on innatism, but that he felt silence was the best policy now that 'innate ideas' had become the subject of derision and scorn in many circles.

Speaking against Urmson's interpretation are the Notebooks, where Berkeley already shows clear signs of discomfort with Locke's famous polemic. At one place, as I pointed out in Chapter 3, Berkeley expresses regret that Locke did not begin the *Essay* with his Third Book – hardly a ringing endorsement of the content of the First Book. In the same entry of his Notebooks, Berkeley goes on to remark that the Third Book 'doesn't agree with' the first two books of the *Essay*. The suggestion therefore seems to be that the *Essay* should have begun with the Third Book precisely because it would have corrected the polemic against innatism and the advocacy of empiricism that characterize Books One and Two.[13]

As we saw in Chapter 3, Berkeley's attention had been caught by the remarks Locke makes about 'particles' in chapter 7 of Book Three of the *Essay*, where the English empiricist had conceded that we may use words to meaningfully refer to acts of the mind without attaching any idea to them. No doubt, Berkeley saw Locke's concession on particles as subversive of his own empiricism for it bypasses Locke's internal sense of reflection which represents our mental operations by idea. The implication of the meaningfulness of particles is that we have a more direct awareness of our active selves than Locke had allowed in Book Two of the *Essay*. It is this direct knowledge of the self and its acts which is marked by the technical term 'notion' in Berkeley's later philosophy and which, I wish to show, has some affinity with innatist theory.

Berkeley's comments about the relative merit of the individual books of Locke's *Essay* comes soon after his only comment on innatism in the early philosophy. It is unequivocal. 'There are innate Ideas i.e. Ideas created with us.'[14] One might think that this statement would trouble empiricist interpreters, but there is little sign of it doing so.[15] One reason is, no doubt, that the entry looks somewhat isolated – a strange one-off that has no lasting significance in Berkeley's thought. Another is that – at a push – an empiricist reading can be found that would neutralize the ostensible endorsement of innatism here as deflationary, almost ironic. Berkeley, according to this view, is saying only that there must have been some ideas in the mind at the beginning of our experience and so we might as well call those 'innate'.[16]

Perhaps there is some prima facie justification for not putting too much weight on this endorsement of innatism. Remarks in the Notebooks are sometimes in conflict with one another and there are apparent changes of mind, especially on the subject of spirit. However, I believe that when we take this comment about innatism together with the comments that immediately follow it in the Notebooks, it does seem likely that Berkeley was questioning the framework of concept empiricism at this point in the earliest phase of his development. However, before I make the case for this interpretation, I need to say more about the doctrine of innatism itself.

Two forms of innatism

If we are to understand the relation of Berkeley's thought to innatism, we should be aware that there were various versions of the doctrine current at the time he was writing. In particular, it is important to distinguish between two kinds of innatism which I shall call 'crude' and 'refined innatism'.

The crude version is to be found in certain places in Descartes's work. This treated innate ideas as part of the furniture of the mind from its inception. Notoriously, Descartes wrote in the *Meditations* that God stamps the idea of himself on our minds just as 'a craftsman stamps his mark on his handiwork'.[17] It was the view encapsulated in this analogy that was most often the target of criticism and that was seized upon by Descartes's early opponents such as Gassendi, Hobbes and (the pseudonymous) Hyperaspistes. Locke, too, focused much, though certainly not all, of his polemical energies on combatting crude innatism,[18] and he first introduces innate notions with a parallel analogy, describing them as 'Characters, as it were stamped on the Mind of Man'.[19] No doubt with remarks like this in mind, William King, Berkeley's fellow Dubliner, noted that 'he [Locke] will allow no idea innate but such as a man brings coined in his mind like a shilling'.[20]

In Descartes's replies to the empiricist objections of Gassendi and Hobbes, and then at greater length in the 'Comments on a Certain Broadsheet', we see a more refined version of innatism emerging. He now says that innate notions do not actually exist in the mind *ab initio*, but merely have the potential to be there. Descartes then explains how this potentiality is actualized in our becoming aware of our own nature as a 'thinking thing'. This refined version involves two, related, modifications of the doctrine. Firstly, by being a dispositional account it asserts only that under the right conditions innate content can be summoned up and made the actual object of thought. Secondly, innatism is now tied to the very definition of the mind as a *res cogitans*, and to the clear and distinct idea of our essence that Descartes thinks we can have. On this view, to perceive my own spiritual essence is to fully understand the content of certain notions like 'thought', 'substance', 'cause' and 'self'. In light of this, we can understand why, in 'Comments on a Certain Broadsheet', Descartes goes as far as to equate innate ideas with 'the mind's own faculty of thinking'.[21]

Descartes's refined version of innatism appears, however, in somewhat marginal places in his *oeuvre*, and even where it is found it is not clearly distinguished from a sweeping version of the dispositional theory that would treat all ideas – both sensory and intellectual – in the mind as innate.[22] A more definite and developed statement of refined innatism is to be found in Leibniz's mature writings. It is advanced in most detail in the *New Essays*, but also, briefly, in a number of other later texts including the *Principles of Nature and Grace* and the *Monadology*.[23] On reading Locke's attack on crude innatism, Leibniz had clearly felt an injustice was being done to the doctrine. He thus set about developing a version that would be impervious to the arguments of the *Essay*.

Leibniz's presentation of his refined from of innatism is characterized by rhetorical finesse. He first asks us to allow one exception to the principle *nihil est in intellectu quod non prius fuerit in sensu* – our idea of the soul or intellect itself.[24] That surely cannot be derived from sense. But the exception turns out to be the thin end of a wedge for, as Leibniz goes on to argue, an innate idea of the soul provides us with the key to other concepts which can be gained from reflection on our own mind. The soul, after all, 'includes being, substance, one, same, cause, perception, reasoning, and many other notions which the senses cannot provide'.[25] An array of intellectual and metaphysical concepts is thus unpacked from an awareness of the mind's own nature.

One important way the refined version of innatism in Leibniz differs from the crude version is that innate ideas are not given to us in a special divine dispensation separate from our creation. God needed no extra intention in granting us innate ideas when he created us. Innate notions are part of our essence as thinking, self-reflective, substances, and, in the very act of creating us as such, God granted us a disposition to arrive at these notions. There is no need for any additional divine act of 'stamping', or 'imprinting' of ideas on a mind created innocent of them. Leibniz's version of innatism, therefore, has the distinct advantage of not being, or seeming to be, ad hoc: it allows us to understand why innate knowledge in potentia must be universal to all spiritual beings capable of self-reflection.[26]

The refined understanding of innate ideas has a further advantage in being ontologically parsimonious. It does not postulate a 'treasure-trove' in the mind from where ideas can be brought forth, as Descartes at one place puts it.[27] Such a view would show an unfitting ontological permissiveness, as Malebranche pointed out when he objected that God 'always acts in the simplest ways'.[28] On the refined view, the mind's thinking nature is enough to grant us the means of arriving at these intellectual concepts. There is no extra ontological baggage that might offend against the principle of 'Occam's razor'.[29]

But the refined, self-reflective, view does come with one potential drawback. It seems quite incompatible with the Cartesian view that our concept of geometrical space is innate. It is very hard to see how our innate ideas of *res extensa* could be derived from mere reflection on the thinking self.[30] For Descartes this looks to be a serious problem, and perhaps that is why it is never unequivocally endorsed by him. For Leibniz, however, this would not have been a drawback. He took our notion of space to be a relative one, dependent on prior knowledge of other existents.[31] Nor, of course, would Berkeley worry about the lack of an innate idea of space, for he stresses that all we know of space is derived from our active experience of willed movement in space. The purely intellectual, non-sensory, concept of 'absolute space' is a phantom:

> From absolute space let us take away now the words of the name, and nothing will remain in sense, imagination, or intellect. Nothing else then is denoted by those words than pure privation or negation, *i.e.* mere nothing.[32]

Berkeley and refined innatism

I wish to suggest that Berkeley's doctrine of notions is closely akin to the refined form of innatism that we find most systematically put forward by Leibniz. This is not to assert any influence. The central text in which Leibniz discussed his refined theory of innatism, the *New Essays*, was not published until 1765, more than a decade after Berkeley's death. The *Monadology* and the *Principles of Nature and Grace* saw the light of day earlier – the *Monadology* appeared in Latin in 1721– but they were not written, let alone published, until after the first editions of Berkeley's *Principles* and *Three Dialogues* of 1710 and 1713. Yes, Berkeley would have read Descartes's responses to Hobbes and to Gassendi, where the refined view is intimated. Here, however, the doctrine was not fully expounded, and a decisive influence is most unlikely. My claim is rather that the doctrine of notions represents Berkeley's independent response to Locke's anti-innatist polemic which has noteworthy parallels with that of Leibniz.

The crucial point on which Berkeley's doctrine of notions and refined innatism agree is that the semantic content of certain central intellectual elements, including mind, cause and substance, is not to be found in the data of sense, nor is it to be abstracted or constructed therefrom. Berkeley, like Leibniz, explains how our access to these elements is made possible by a non-sensory attention to the nature of the mind itself. This is part and parcel of his view that our knowledge of mind, causation and substance is not mediated 'by idea', since all ideas – and only ideas – have a strictly sensory basis on his view. Berkeley remarked in his Notebooks that 'by Idea I mean any sensible or imaginable thing',[33] and that is the use of the term which he employs throughout his writings up to, and including, *Siris*, where he confirms that 'there are properly no *ideas*, or passive objects, in the mind but what were derived from sense'.[34]

It is therefore no wonder that in *De motu* Berkeley writes that an understanding of cause cannot be gained from ideas, but only when we 'meditate' on 'incorporeal things', and he treats the concept of causation thus acquired as subject-matter for 'First Philosophy' or metaphysics.[35] Nor is it surprising that he derides the sensory, corporeal understanding of substance as a quasi-spatial support, standing under the properties of things. Substance must be understood in a quite different way to the suggestions of sense and imagination: not as a support, but as a perceiver and an agent.[36]

In *Siris*, where Berkeley openly uses the language of innatism, he claims that 'mind, knowledge and notions, either in habit, or in act, always go together'. The mind *is constituted* by the knowledge involved in notions, a view he finds in the writings of Parmenides and Plato.[37] This does not mean that innate knowledge must always be actually remarked upon by the mind – the knowledge may be 'in habit' or implicit – but it does mean that such knowledge is available to the mind at all times. 'This notion seemeth somewhat different from that of innate ideas, as understood by those moderns who have attempted to explode them,' he writes, indicating that he looked upon Locke's famous polemic, focusing on the crude version of innatism, as little more than a red herring.[38]

Now it is time to return to the endorsement of innate ideas in the Notebooks at 649. This comment is one of a group of six entries, all marked with an 'S' in the left-hand margin, indicating they are about spirit. The first four in the group seem to represent a connected episode of thought. The three that follow the assertion of innate content at 649 make a series of forthright denials of Locke's view that thought is an operation of the mind, not its essence, and of Locke's related claim that the mind can exist without thinking 'in Sleep and trances'.[39] Here are the entries in question:

S	There are innate Ideas i.e. Ideas created with us.	649
S	Locke seems to be mistaken when he says thought is not essential to the mind.	650
S	Certainly the mind always & constantly thinks & we know this too in Sleep & trances the mind exists not there is no time no succession of Ideas.	651
S	To say the mind exists' without thinking is a Contradiction, nonsense, nothing.	652

The connection of sections 650–2 with the initial entry 649 becomes intelligible in the light of the self-reflexive version of innatism, which I am calling the 'refined view'. On this view, after all, innate content is available to us because we can have knowledge of our essence as thinking beings.[40] If we were to be in the dark about our own essence, as Locke would have it, we would be deprived of this source of innate content. Moreover, Locke's reason for denying that we know the mind to be essentially a thinking thing is precisely the occurrence of 'Sleep and trances' when the mind persists without thinking. It seems likely, therefore, that this cluster of entries is more than a miscellany of reservations about Locke's philosophy. It is a connected set of thoughts guided, I suggest, by an attachment to something like Leibniz's understanding of innatism, or, as *Siris* §309 would have it, to the thesis that 'mind, knowledge and notions, either in habit, or in act, always go together'.

The affinity of Berkeley's doctrine of notions with Leibniz's version of innatism is also evident in the central examples that the two thinkers give us of their non-sensory notions. In the *Monadology*, Leibniz writes that 'by thinking of ourselves, we think of being, of substance, of simples and composites, of the immaterial – and, by realizing that what is limited in us is limitless in him, of God himself'.[41] This list is augmented in other places, with 'action', 'virtue', 'perception' and 'cause' being included in the *New Essays*.[42] Most of these examples also appear, in one place or another, among Berkeley's examples of notions. That is not, of course, to say that there are no differences. Leibniz, unlike Berkeley, was concerned with the innateness of temporal concepts, such as 'duration' and 'change', while Berkeley takes the Augustinian step of including emotions among notions.

Possible objections considered

Let us consider some potential objections to our linking of Berkeley's doctrine of notions with the refined version of innatism. Firstly, it might be said that Berkeley's position exhibits a closer resemblance to the crude version of innatism than to its more refined cousin because notions are ever-present to the mind, which is always active. It hardly seems consistent of Berkeley to talk of notions of self, substance and causation as being *potentially* in the mind, since if the mind is essentially active, there can be no periods in our mental life when there is no thinking, and therefore no periods when these notions are not *actually* present to the active mind.

In responding to this objection we might first point out that when Berkeley himself adopts a favourable attitude to innatist doctrine in public, particularly in passages of *Alciphron* and the Sermon 'On the Will of God', he is primarily interested in the notion of God.[43] This notion is not present to the mind from its beginning, but requires reason and reflection for the mind to become aware of it, as we shall see in Chapter 8. Berkeley's account of the notion of God, and of some other notions (e.g. of other finite minds and of moral concepts), should certainly be given a dispositional account in the spirit of the refined version of innatism.

But that still leaves notions of the self, the mind, causation and substance, which seem to have been permanently with us from the beginning of our experience. In relation to these, Berkeley seems to think that one requires attention to one's own active being in order to be aware of them. In the course of explaining his Master Argument, as we saw in Chapter 3, Berkeley tells us that the mind is apt to 'take no notice of itself',[44] and this surely means that the notion of the mind, though it is always potentially accessible to us, need not be the actual subject of awareness from the mind's beginning. We are not fully aware of ourselves and our own acts when we are immersed in sensible ideas.

A second objection would point to the undeniable fact that the content of Berkeley's notions is still gained from experience in the most general sense of the word.[45] Is this not enough to make him a concept empiricist? Was not Locke's fundamental empiricist claim that 'all the materials of Reason and Knowledge' are derived 'from Experience'?[46] Thus Anthony Grayling writes: 'The signal point is that without experience as such we do not come by notions; so Berkeley's empiricism is unequivocal.'[47]

The trouble with this objection is that the same may be said of the refined version of innatism that we have been discussing. That too says that innate concepts emerge in the course of experience as the thinking subject becomes aware of its own nature, and Leibniz is happy to talk about 'experience' of the self in this connection.[48] Grayling's broad understanding of empiricism therefore risks bringing Leibniz into the empiricist fold. Experience is too general a concept to usefully distinguish empiricism from rationalism – a Platonist appeals to experience of the Forms, and mysticism involves experience of a supernatural reality.

At this point some might throw up their arms in exasperation and say that refined innatism and empiricism can no longer be usefully separated from one another, and that the distinction between innatists and empiricists has been erased. But I wish to use the term 'empiricism' in the narrow sense of conceptual empiricism that we outlined in the introduction. On this view empiricism requires that intellectual concepts be derived from the content of sense experience or something strongly analogous to it, such as reflection construed as an 'internal sense'; and this is exactly what Berkeley denies is the case with the concepts of self, substance, causation, unity and goodness, and the other concepts which we have notions of. So a real contrast can be made between Berkeley's position and that of empiricists, such as Gassendi and Locke, who thought that all the contents of intellectual thought are derived from sense-experience or from experience that is strongly analogous to sense-experience (Gassendi's *'le sens intime'* and Locke's 'internal sense' of reflection).[49]

The specificity of Berkeley's notions

But there does remain one significant difference between Berkeley's appeal to notions and the refined innatism of Descartes and Leibniz. I would suggest that it is this difference that makes Berkeley's position neither innatist nor empiricist, but rather a coincidence of the two opposing views, as suggested in *Siris* §308. Although Descartes and Leibniz reject the empiricist model of self-knowledge, resisting any attempt to treat self-knowledge as involving images or a quasi-sensory faculty, they do still talk of a *perception* of the self, and of the other ideas that are deemed innate. This is strikingly put in Descartes's Second Meditation, where the meditator describes his liberation from sensory perceptions and his coming on the pure idea of his self in the following way:

> I thus realise that none of the things that the imagination enables me to grasp is at all relevant to this knowledge of myself which I possess, and that the mind must therefore be more carefully diverted from such things if it is to perceive its own nature as distinctly as possible [*ut suam ipsa naturam quam distinctissime percipiat*].[50]

Here Descartes, at the same time as he dismisses any role for images in conceiving of the self, clearly affirms that self-knowledge is a *perception* of one's own nature. Self-awareness involves a purely intellectual representation and is thus quite distinct from the images of the bodily senses, but it is still constituted by the perception of an item that stands immediately before the mind. Descartes, whether consciously or not, treats self-reflection as in some fundamental way parallel to the intellectual idea of space, in which an idea of the pure intellect is beheld by the mind. Such a view implies a split between perceiving subject and perceived object. The paradoxical character of such a mental act is palpable when applied to the self. If we treat self-knowledge as a form of perception, then – however intellectual and non-sensory we make this mental act – it threatens to be self-defeating, as the self, *qua* perceiver, eludes its own perception. It is as if, to use Gilbert Ryle's analogy, one is trying to jump on the shadow of one's own head.[51]

Leibniz, too, does not hesitate to use the language of ideas to assert his version of innatism. Though he may distinguish between perception and apperception, the latter remains a form of perception in the broadest sense, and it involves our perceiving ourselves and our thoughts by idea. Leibniz, who was as committed to the 'new way of ideas' as Descartes and Locke before him, treated ideas as the 'immediate objects of thinking'. There is no attempt, on Leibniz's part, to make room for understanding or knowledge that is unmediated by idea, as Berkeley's doctrine of notions requires.[52]

Evidence of the gap between Berkeley and Leibniz in this respect is the surprising extent to which Leibniz can go along with Locke's theory of reflection. While Berkeley dismisses the theory of reflection as a 'grand Mistake', Leibniz is more forgiving. He sees in Locke's theory of reflection the unwitting beginnings of an innatist theory. The point is to go further than Locke, and attribute other ideas to this inner sense, including ideas of the mind itself and its substance. Leibniz writes:

> It is very true that our perceptions of ideas come either from the external senses or from the internal sense, which one might call 'reflection'. But this faculty of reflection is not confined only to the operations of the spirit [as Locke argues]. It extends to the mind itself, and it is through perceiving the mind that we perceive substance.[53]

Leibniz here is clearly at ease with the thought that we perceive our own mind, and its substantiality. As he writes elsewhere, we have no knowledge (*notitia*) of substance 'except from our intimate experience of ourselves when we perceive the self [*cum percipimus to Ego*]'.[54] While it would be wrong to see this as an endorsement of the empiricist 'sense' of reflection, because Leibniz, like

Descartes, is clearly thinking of an intellectual perception, he does think there is significant common ground between him and Locke – a shared concern with a peculiar species of inner perception.

Berkeley stands opposed to Locke and Leibniz on the question of whether self-reflection should be understood as a form of perception. His notions are neither analogous to perceptions nor do we catch sight of them in any quasi-perceptual way. Nor indeed are they objects of thought at all. Berkeley's notions are not what Kant later termed *Vorstellungen*; that is, mental representations that have their place (*stellen*) before (*vor*) our minds.[55] Notions avoid the fundamental duality of mind and representation – of a subject regarding an object – that *Vorstellungen* would implicitly affirm.[56] Notions are knowledge that we have *through* our being active. Berkeley's theory claims that we, as active beings, are aware of our operations through exercising them: by 'a kind of inner consciousness' (*conscientia quadam interna*), as he puts it in *De motu*.[57] There is no *perception* of the self as an object: rather it is our own mental doings that reveal our active nature.

'To have an idea is all one as to perceive', Berkeley tells us early in the *Principles*.[58] Thus his repeated denial that we have an idea of spirit amounts to a conscious rejection of any form of perception of our active spiritual being.[59] The knowledge involved is of a different species. By rejecting the perceptual model of self-knowledge, Berkeley is able to bring about the synthesis described at *Siris* §308:

> [Aristotle] held that the mind of man was a *tabula rasa*, and that there were no innate ideas. Plato, on the contrary, held original ideas in the mind; that is, notions which never were or can be in the sense, such as being, beauty, goodness, likeness, parity. Some, perhaps, may think the truth to be this: that there are properly no *ideas*, or passive objects, in the mind but what were derived from sense: but that there are also besides these her own acts or operations; such are *notions*.

The synthesis outlined here takes both conceptual empiricism and rationalist innatism to express one side of the truth, once their scope has been appropriately specified. Conceptual empiricism holds true for what we can perceive. Perceptions – that is, mental objects or ideas – are always either sensory, or derived from sense experience. Berkeley's view remains the same as in the Notebooks, where, as quoted above, he treats idea to mean 'any sensible or imaginable thing'. The only objects that the mind can have before it are sensory, or the reawakened objects of sense in imagination and memory. This means that he can endorse the scholastic principle '*nihil est in intellectu quod non fuit prius in sensu*', as long as stress is placed on the 'in' of '*in intellectu*', so that the scope of the principle is limited to objects (ideas) *in* the mind.[60]

None of these empirically derived ideas, however, gives us an understanding of self, causal power or substance. Nor do they give us an understanding of parity, likeness or of the moral and aesthetic notions that Berkeley mentions in *Siris*. To explain our grasp of these elements – so central to the rationalist tradition – Berkeley appeals to our exercise of spiritual powers, and it is here that empiricism is found to fall short. Our intuitive grasp of spirit, substance, causal power, likeness and value, is not derived from sense, but is internal to the mind's own active being. As long as the scope of rationalism is limited to our mental activities, and does not take in our ideas – as innatists had traditionally claimed – the doctrine is found to hold true.

It is no wonder that, when Berkeley identifies his philosophy most closely with Platonism in *Siris*, he stresses the active nature of the forms. The forms for Berkeley are not archetypes of natural objects, or their 'perspective-free representations'.[61] Nor does he go the way of his early modern predecessor, Malebranche, who had the mind 'seeing' quasi-Platonic ideas in an intimately present God. Instead knowledge of the forms amounts to an active influence on us, a rule for our behaviour, or 'a guide to govern' our conduct. Plato's term 'idea', Berkeley states, 'doth not merely signify an inert inactive object of the understanding, but is used as synonymous with αἴτιον and ἀρχή, cause and principle'.[62] It is by returning to Plato, therefore, that Berkeley can correct the innatism of his own times, built on a Cartesian, perceptual understanding of idea.

The inseparability of notions from ideas

There is a further feature of Berkeley's doctrine of notions that separates it from the innatist tradition. An innate idea, as the object of a peculiar form of perception, is in principle a self-contained object of the mind's attention. We can make sense of our attention being fully occupied with innate content, and this seems to be what Descartes has in mind when the narrator of the

Meditations initially perceives his own immaterial self, excluding all the imagery of sense. Innate content is, after all, taken to be in an antagonistic relation with the content of sense because it is fundamentally the same kind of thing – the object of mental perception. While the mind can be fully occupied with sensory ideas, when purged of them it can turn itself instead towards a contemplation of the objects of pure intellect.

Berkeley's notions, on the other hand, are unthinkable without the co-presence of ideas of sense which are the objects of the mental activities concerned. Notions and ideas have a *complementary* relation since operations require objects on which to operate. Without ideas of sense, or their derivatives in imagination and memory, the mind would be bereft of content and would be unable to think, or to be in any way active. Thus, notions can only ever be *one* component of our experience. When Berkeley writes, at *Siris* §308, that 'there are properly no *ideas*, or passive objects, in the mind but what were derived from sense: but that there are also besides these her own acts or operations; such are *notions*', he implies that ideas are objects structured and formed by mental acts or notions. Ideas and notions, therefore, are mutually dependent.

We might make a comparison with another philosopher who, as we have already seen, also offered a non-perceptual account of knowledge of our own mental activities, Johann Gottlieb Fichte. Fichte tells us that an 'intellectual intuition' of our acting selves can never be a self-enclosed act, occurring in isolation from sense intuition. 'I cannot discover myself to be acting without also discovering some object upon which I act; and I discover this object by means of sensory intuition.' Thus, as Fichte goes on to affirm, the act of intellectual intuition is no 'isolated consciousness' but is necessarily accompanied by the objects of sensory experience.[63]

It has been the suggestion of this chapter that the perceptual model of cognition, which was part and parcel of the 'new way of ideas', made possible the clear divide in early modern philosophy between empiricism and rationalism. 'Contraries', as J. S. Mill reminds us, are 'the things which are farthest from one another *in the same kind*'.[64] The contrast of empiricism and innatism is made possible by a shared perceptual model of knowledge – they are 'the same kind' in this respect. Berkeley, by rejecting ideas of spirit and its activities, and thus abandoning the perceptual model of cognition for the inner, can no longer be usefully presented as either empiricist or innatist.

5

Sense perception: A passive or an active power?

The time has come to have a close look at Berkeley's understanding of sense perception. We find him claiming, in certain places, particularly in his early works, that sense perception is an utterly passive affair. This would seem to make problems for our interpretation as it would deny the complementarity of idea and notion that we spoke of at the close of Chapter 4. It would suggest that mental activity is not required for us to have sensory perceptions or ideas. Moreover, this raises the question of how a passive process can be ascribed to the purely active self, known by notion, and thus how sense perception can be thought of as an operation of mind at all? In this chapter, I will investigate Berkeley's understanding of sense perception and attempt to determine its consistency with the claim that spirit is essentially and continually active.

The passivity of perception

A passive view of sense perception is stated in the *Principles* where, for example, we read:

> When in broad day-light I open my eyes, it is not in my power to choose whether I shall see or no, or to determine what particular objects shall present themselves to my view; and so likewise as to the hearing and other senses, the ideas imprinted on them are not creatures of my will.[1]

This statement is important for Berkeley because the independence of perception from my will is a key criterion for distinguishing ideas of real things from products of the imagination. The ideas of imagination I can, after all, 'excite in my mind at pleasure' by an act of volition.[2] In this, Berkeley is following Descartes for whom the fact that we are acted upon in perception is the key to proving the existence of an external world that causes the ideas of perception.[3] True, for Berkeley the immediate external cause of the ideas is a spiritual one, whereas for Descartes it is a material one, but in both cases the fact that ideas of perception are 'produced without my cooperation and often even against my will', as Descartes puts it, is proof of the *externality* of the cause.[4]

The *Three Dialogues* (1713) goes further than the passage from the *Principles* just quoted. Here we find a denial of the very possibility of any active element in sense perception on the part of the subject. In the First Dialogue, Hylas and Philonous appear to agree on the narrow thesis that not only is perception a passive process, it is *nothing more than* a passive process. There is no *act* in perceiving at all. It is this view of perception that, I think, creates difficulties for Berkeley's view of the spiritual self which he has characterized as 'one simple, undivided, active being'.[5] It becomes very hard to understand how the *purely* passive state of perception can belong to a self which has been defined as an essentially active being. So let us begin by examining this claim about perception in the passage of the First Dialogue itself.[6]

A Two-Component View of perception?

In the passage in question, Hylas is pursuing his ill-fated defence of matter. Having just seen the distinction between primary and secondary qualities dismantled by Philonous, his immaterialist opponent, Hylas has now conceded that primary qualities cannot be separated, in either experience or thought, from secondary qualities. He thus comes to accept that 'all sensible qualities are alike to be denied existence without the mind'.[7] Now, in an attempt to regain the initiative, and to defend the existence of material things, Hylas turns to the nature of sense perception itself. He distinguishes between an act of perception, which (rather confusingly perhaps) he calls 'sensation', and the passive object of perception.[8] While the active sensation cannot exist without the mind, he argues, the object of the sensation may.

The reasoning here may seem at first sight paradoxical. One would have thought that the need for an act of sensation makes the object of perception *more* dependent on mind and its activity. However, Hylas's claim is that the mental act in question renders an otherwise independent object present to our minds. The object is thus only contingently connected with our perception of it. It is not itself constituted by the perceptual act, but rather it is a component of perception that is detachable from the act, and which might 'belong to an unthinking thing'.[9]

An analogy with the act of picking up a stone might help. The fact that I must actively reach out and grasp the stone demonstrates that it is quite able to sit in the environment prior to my reaching for it, and is also able to return to that environment when I discard it. If no such act was necessary on my part the object would somehow be part of me, just as my hand is part of my own body and is not, therefore, something that I need to reach for. The Two-Component View of perception, as I shall call it, separates the act of perception ('sensation') from the object perceived, so that that object is not constituted by my perception of it, just as the stone is not constituted by my reaching hand.

Hylas's new attempt to make sense of an external material object is, we might notice, perfectly neutral about the distinction between primary and secondary qualities. Hylas hopes to invoke a common-sense understanding of the physical object perceived. Indeed, in the example that Hylas offers of perceiving the red and yellow colours of a tulip, he is clearly not making any appeal to bodies characterized by primary qualities alone. The argument rather distinguishes between *all* perceptual qualities *qua* objects of perception, on the one hand, and the act of the mind perceiving them, on the other. The defence hinges on there being these two separable components in what goes under the term perception: act and object. The Two-Component View allows an ontologically independent object to become cognitively present to my conscious mind, but also to be detached or absent from it at other times.

Philonous's critical reaction to the Two-Component View focuses on the active component. When we try to define this act of sensation, he argues, it is found to be utterly diaphanous. The mental act of perceiving is not experienced. It is a perfect phantom. The actions associated with perception are confined to acts of volition that govern the movement of our bodies as we position ourselves to best receive perceptual data. I cannot, in addition, actively determine whether or not I see a bright light in the sky when my eyes are open and my head is tilted upward towards the sun; or whether or not I smell a certain odour when I hold a flower to my nose and breathe in. There is no active component in the perception itself.

Hylas's act of perceiving thus melts away and we are left with only the immediate object of perception – the passive idea. Philonous concludes with a rhetorical question that leaves Hylas lost for words:

> Since therefore you are in the very perception of light and colours altogether passive, what is become of that action you were speaking of, as an ingredient in every sensation?

The two interlocutors seem to have come to the view which was later expressed by Gilbert Ryle:

> If I descry a hawk, I find the hawk but I do not find my seeing of the hawk. My seeing of the hawk seems to be a queerly transparent sort of process, transparent in that while a hawk is detected, nothing else is detected answering to the verb in 'see a hawk'.[10]

The problems with a passive view of sense perception

By denying the Two-Component View, and affirming the passivity of perception, Philonous is able to block Hylas's renewed attempt to defend matter, but the passive view of sense perception would seem to pose problems for Berkeley's own idealist position. Most dangerously for idealism, an unbridgeable divide between willing and perceiving opens up. Perception now seems to be no more than the presence of inert ideas, but it is no longer clear how one can maintain – as an idealist must – that these various sensible qualities or ideas are '*in the mind*'. For how can an idea – a passive perceived object – ever become attached to a purely willing being and be thought to be *in* it? This problem is made particularly acute by Berkeley's insistence that the mind is indivisible and therefore active *simpliciter*.

Some commentators have seen this problem as fatal to Berkeley's attempt to make sense of the self. It has even been suggested, by Charles McCracken, that it may have been 'prudent good sense' which led him to abandon the second part of the *Principles* where he had planned to expound his view of spiritual substance. McCracken despairs of ever providing an answer, on Berkeley's behalf, to the question of 'how a thing that is perfectly simple and unitary can be simultaneously in such radically different states as those of actively willing and passively perceiving'.[11] In other words, Berkeley's dualism of passive idea and active spirit is too sharply drawn to leave us any hope of combining the two disparate categories in one mind.

There is also a second problem for Berkeley. If sense perception is purely passive, then what will become of the mind in those intervals of time when it is *only* perceiving or contemplating ideas? The very nature of the soul as an active principle will be suspended, and thus the mind or self must cease to exist. One is reminded of a parallel problem with Descartes's definition of the mind as 'a thinking thing' (*res cogitans*). As was quickly pointed out by Gassendi, and later by Locke, this definition of the mind entails that we are constantly thinking, even in fainting fits and dreamless sleep. Descartes agreed that we are indeed thinking in such states, but argued that the memory retains no trace. As is well known, Berkeley, who also thinks that the mind is continually active, solves this Cartesian problem by embracing a subjective theory of time. But Berkeley would now seem to have nothing to offer – however *ad hoc* – to ensure that the mind persists through a purely passive episode of conscious perception.[12]

Now, unlike McCracken, I think that these difficulties can be dealt with on Berkeley's behalf. But to do so we shall need to take a close look at his philosophical development. I wish to suggest that in the first edition of the *Three Dialogues* Berkeley was in a transitional phase of his thinking about spirit, and a stable and coherent position had yet to be attained. With his primary goal of making the non-existence of matter compelling to the reader, Berkeley had put arguments into the mouths of his fictional partners in dialogue, arguments which do not reflect the full details of his own thinking about perception and his understanding of spiritual substance. I wish to argue that certain views, already visible in his early philosophy, are developed in Berkeley's later thought making for a more consistent position. This position, while hinted at in certain comments in the original edition of the *Three Dialogues*, comes properly into view only in the 1734 edition.

Mental activity as willing

Before I discuss the development of Berkeley's thought on sense perception and how it remedies the problems that an utterly passive view presents, we must first gain a clearer idea of the steps that have led Hylas and Philonous to the conclusion that perception is absolutely passive. Instrumental, here, is a narrow and reductive conception of mental activity:

Philonous: When is the mind said to be active?

Hylas: When it produces, puts an end to, or changes anything.

Philonous: Can the mind produce, discontinue, or change anything but by an act of the will?

Hylas: It cannot.[13]

There are two reductive moves visible in this short exchange. The first (actually coming second in the passage quoted) is to reduce all mental activity to willing; the second is to reduce all willing to 'producing, discontinuing and changing anything'. It is these two moves, working in tandem, that make it impossible to conceive of an active component in perception itself. The only kind of mental activity now envisaged are the acts of will that position the body, or the sense organ, in a suitable place, with the appropriate posture, to receive the sensory input.

Strangely, we know that Berkeley was aware of the controversial character of each of these reductive moves. In his Notebooks, after all, he had entertained richer conceptions of both mental activity and of willing. True, we do find Berkeley bluntly asserting that 'we cannot possibly conceive any active power but the Will'.[14] But this early comment seems to be overridden by later entries that treat reasoning and understanding (which includes perception) as active – and not purely passive – faculties. In one late entry, Berkeley goes as far as to assert that 'understanding is in some sort an Action'.[15] We also find here a sustained attempt to treat will and understanding as so bound up with one another that 'volitions and ideas cannot be severed' and 'either [one] cannot be possibly without the other'.[16] As we shall see presently, Berkeley returns to something like this unified view in his final philosophical work, *Siris*.

Just as controversial is the very limited conception of willing that the passage in the First Dialogue advances. Willing is reduced to discrete acts of producing, destroying and changing. The acts of willing that Hylas and Philonous go on to discuss are – what's more – those that govern *bodily* movement as the perceiver seeks to gain perceptions of sight and smell.[17] The picture evoked is of a will intervening – in staccato acts of volition – to start, stop or redirect the acting body. Nothing is said about the willing of a *continuation* of an action or state, let alone of the continuation of a *mental* action or state.

The inadequacy of the conception of will in this passage of the First Dialogue is further exacerbated by a failure to consider forbearance. Forbearance, we should remember, is different to the willed 'stopping' or 'ending' an action that has already begun. Forbearance is an exertion of the will which prevents an action from even starting. Forbearance in this sense, which is stressed in the work of both John Locke and Anthony Collins, is closely related to the power of attention as it allows one to resist the various forms of distraction and temptation that come one's way.[18]

So Hylas's conception of willing is simplified and unsatisfactory in these different ways, and this will inevitably undermine the case made for the passivity of perception in the First Dialogue. Someone regarding a tulip, after all, must focus attention on their visual sensation if they are to take in the red and yellow colours of the flower.[19] If one is distracted, the perception may not be properly registered. An extreme case of this is described by Descartes when 'the soul is distracted by an ecstasy or deep contemplation, we see that the whole body remains without sensation, even though it has various objects touching it'.[20] Locke seems to have a similar state of rapture in mind when he refers to the state of 'Extasy', comparing it to 'dreaming with the Eyes open'.[21] Locke also goes on to describe the varying degrees of attention, the lowest of which allows ideas to 'pass almost quite unregarded, faint shadows, that make no Impression'.[22]

The inadequacy of Berkeley's conception of will here raises the question of whether this passage from the First Dialogue can be treated as the definitive statement of his view of mental activity. Apart from anything else, it is Hylas and Philonous, not Berkeley, who concur on the narrow conception of volition we are considering, and so the conclusion here may be a provisional one, or even one meant *ad hominem*. For another thing, as we have seen, Berkeley provides richer notions of will and mental activity in other places in his writings. To return to the Notebooks, Berkeley is ready to acknowledge a role for willing in every seemingly passive mental state, including states of perception, when he writes of the continuous 'acquiescing' of volition that any perception implies, and thus he feels able to claim that 'While I exist or have any Idea I am eternally, constantly willing'.[23] More importantly for us, he also puts forward a much broader understanding of mental activity in the third edition of the *Three Dialogues* in a passage I shall now turn to.

The act of unity in Berkeley's later philosophy

As is well known, the text of the *Three Dialogues* that Berkeley ultimately left us represents two different stages in his philosophical development that are separated by more than twenty years. When we read the *Three Dialogues* we are reading a book originally written in Berkeley's late twenties with changes or interpolations introduced by his (almost) fifty-year-old self. There is a clear sign, in those changes, that the author no longer recognizes the passivity of perception thesis as the final word (if he ever really did). In one new passage on the spiritual self, Philonous is made to say the following:

> How often must I repeat, that I know or am conscious of my own being; and that I myself am not my ideas, but somewhat else, a thinking active principle that perceives, knows, wills, and operates about ideas. I know that I, one and the same self, perceive both colours and sounds: that a colour cannot perceive a sound, nor a sound a colour: that I am therefore one individual principle, distinct from colour and sound; and, for the same reason, from all other sensible things and inert ideas.

The first sentence in this passage strongly suggests that perceiving and knowing, as well as willing, are modes of a 'thinking active principle'. When Philonous says 'I am a thinking active principle that perceives, knows, wills, and operates about ideas', the message conveyed is that perceiving, knowing, willing and operating about ideas all equally share in the active nature of the spirit.

The argument which then follows, despite the brevity of its presentation, is sufficiently clear in outline. It draws on this more inclusive notion of activity in affirming an act of unification in sense perception. Philonous considers how the mind takes in sensory perceptions in diverse modalities – vision and hearing in the example. He claims that only the thinking active principle, which he has just characterized, can bestow on sense-experience this unity. The alternative would be for sensible ideas themselves to create the unity by perceiving each other, a possibility which is at once dismissed as absurd. So,

Philonous concludes, the self must be treated as 'one individual principle' that is separate from ideas. This simple active self combines different sensible modalities in a single experience. Philonous's reference to the *inertness* of ideas suggests that they are disqualified from having this role because the unity of consciousness is an active process.

Now, this thought about the unifying power of the mind is not completely new in Berkeley's philosophy, but can be traced back to reflections on unity and number expressed in the Notebooks, the *Essay on Vision* and the *Principles*. In Notebook B (entry 110), Berkeley had written that:

> Number not in bodies it being the creature of the mind depending entirely on it's consideration & being more or less as the mind pleases.

In the *Essay on Vision*, Berkeley added to this thought. The number and unity of visible things, we are told, arises as the mind 'parcels out' ideas into 'distinct collections', 'bundling [them] up together'. A person born blind on receiving sight would lack the ability to 'parcel out' visual ideas according to the patterns of tactile associations. That person's ideas of colour and light would 'crowd into his mind' together, and they would not 'distribute into sundry distinct combinations' the different ideas of surrounding bodies. When viewing a human being that person would lack the orientation to tell 'up' from 'down', or head from foot. The visual experience in question would be inchoate and thoroughly confused.[24]

In this passage of the *Essay on Vision*, it is true, Berkeley was talking about ideas in a single sense modality, vision, and not in more than one as he does in the addition to the Third Dialogue we are concerned with. But the underlying thought is the same: the objects of sense perception do not have intrinsic unity; unity is bestowed on them as an active mind unites a plurality of content into an object. Only thus can we arrive at units, and thence at numbers of units.

In the *Principles*, the thought about number is given prominence. The number of the things known to sense arises from their active categorisation by the mind. As Berkeley puts it:

> Number is so visibly relative, and dependent on men's understanding, that it is strange to think how anyone should give it an absolute existence without the mind. We say one book, one page, one line; all these are equally units, though some contain several of the others. And in each instance it is plain,

the unit relates to some particular combination of ideas arbitrarily put together by the mind.[25]

At this point, we might remark on an anomaly pertaining to the 1713 edition of the *Three Dialogues*. In his discussion of primary qualities, Berkeley omits all explicit reference to this active conception of number and unity that we find him so forcefully advocating in the *Principles* three years earlier. This is strange because his arguments against primary qualities – of which the active account of number was an important part – are otherwise expanded in the First Dialogue when compared with the *Principles* and the *Essay on Vision*. So why do Philonous and Hylas have nothing to say about the primary quality of number, or unity, confining their attention to extension, figure, motion, rest and solidity?[26] Perhaps Berkeley decided that the point about number would be just too paradoxical for the more popular readership that he sought to engage by using the dialogue form. Or did Berkeley omit reference to number in 1713 because he realized that his thinking in this regard would be dissonant with the passivity of perception thesis advanced in the passage that immediately follows the critique of the primary–secondary distinction?

The exact state of Berkeley's thinking about number and unity in 1713 is not quite clear, a point I shall return to. But what is clear is that the view Berkeley adumbrates in the *Principles* and before, is resurgent in his later philosophy where it is one of the principal philosophical topics of *Siris*.[27] Here we are told that

> Number is no object of sense: it is an act of the mind. The same thing in a different conception is one or many.[28]

The formulation here is stronger than in the Notebooks and the *Principles*, which treated number as a 'creature of the mind'.[29] The term 'creature' (used in the theological sense of 'creation') indicates something actively produced by the mind but now subsisting there as one of its contents. The shift from 'creature of the mind' to 'act of the mind' suggests that there is never an enduring object of perception or thought that can then be stored and recollected. The number in things is, instead, the result of an ongoing synthetic process, as the mind moulds the data of sense – including the images of imagination and memory – into units. If that unifying activity were to be suspended then the units, and number itself, would also be suspended.

The suggestion that Berkeley has this kind of continuous unifying act in mind is borne out by later sections of *Siris* where he expands on the theme:

> In things sensible and imaginable, as such, there seems to be no unity, nothing that can be called one, prior to all act of the mind; since they, being in themselves aggregates, consisting of parts or compounded of elements, are in effect many.[30]

If 'prior' is read here in a non-temporal, 'logical' sense, then our unified experience of sense and imagination already involves an act of mind. In the section that immediately follows this, Berkeley revisits his earlier critique of primary qualities, reminding us of how 'the moderns' erred in treating number as 'an original primary quality in things', recommending instead the view – ascribed to Aristotle by Themistius – that 'the mind maketh each thing to be one'. He finishes in a neo-Platonist vein:

> The mind, by virtue of her simplicity, conferreth simplicity upon compounded beings. And indeed, it seemeth that the mind, so far forth as person, is individual, therein resembling the divine One by participation, and imparting to other things what itself participates from above.[31]

The picture that emerges from this statement is that the mind, thanks to its intrinsic simplicity, is possessed of unity, and this allows it to lend to the diverse data of sense new unities. The indeterminate plurality of perceptual input is thus transformed into the experience of objects. This, I suggest, is the view which we saw intimated in the 1734 edition of the *Three Dialogues*, published ten years before *Siris*. It means that our perceptual experience of a single and integrated world, made up of individuated objects, is the result of our mind actively participating in that experience. This cannot – for the most part at least – be conscious volitional activity. The activity of the mind is now clearly much wider than what would pass as 'willing' in everyday discourse.

The doctrine expressed here may be compared with Kantian 'synthesis'. Kant's underlying idea is reasonably clear. Synthesis is a process of combination that is actively introduced by the subject in shaping the manifold of intuition. The input of sense would remain hopelessly disparate and fragmented in the absence of synthesis, and would not be a possible object of experience, for experience entails unity. Moreover, synthesis involves the application of intellectual categories that mould the manifold of sense into the objects of the spatio-temporal world we encounter in experience.[32] The same broad characterization may be made of Berkeley's view about unity and number in experience, particularly as he expounds it in *Siris*, in the last phase of his philosophy.

One crucial difference from Kant is that Berkeley treats the unity of experience as grounded in our simple, indivisible self. Kant would reject any such neo-Platonic claim about the metaphysical nature of the soul as symptomatic of a dogmatic 'rational psychology', seeking knowledge beyond the limits of possible experience. Kant, unlike Berkeley, treats the ultimate ground of synthesis – and thus the ground of unity in consciousness – as lying beyond the bounds of possible knowledge.[33] For Berkeley there can be no source of unity other than the simplicity of the soul substance of which we have immediate knowledge or a notion.

Hints of perceptual activity in the *Three Dialogues*

It is time to return to the First Dialogue and to reassess the argument for the passivity of perception. We must bear in mind that the target of Philonous's critique was not so much activity inherent in perceiving, but rather a particular conception of this activity that we have called the Two-Component View. On this view the active component is distinguishable in experience from the passive component, or idea. There is an additive relation between these two components such that the passive part can be severed from the active part and persist in its absence. I believe there are signs that while Berkeley, in the First Dialogue, rejects the Two-Component View outright, he may not wish, even here, to deny a role for mental activity in perception.

Evidence of the activity of mind in perception is apparent when Hylas and Philonous come to discuss 'outness' or distance as it is presented in vision.[34] It becomes clear that the light and colours of the tulip, which were treated as passively given in perception, are now put into a broader context of distance vision, which is found to be the product of mental activity. Philonous, drawing on Berkeley's theory of vision, explains our visual perception of distance thus:

> From the ideas you actually perceive by sight, you have by experience learned to collect what other ideas you will (according to the standard order of Nature) be affected with, after such a certain succession of time and motion.[35]

It may seem that I am, in a single instant, immediately seeing the distance of the tulip, but that is an illusion. In fact, I am judging that distance by using my past experience in other sense-modalities, particularly touch, to anticipate the felt effort of moving towards the flower. This means that if I see a tulip at a certain distance – as, surely, I must – it is the result of my being mentally active. I am assessing the distance by drawing on my previous experience with motor-sensation when walking, or reaching, across the space between me and the flower. I am actively 'collecting' these experienced connections, and my perception of distance is really a result of this implicit mental activity.

The passivity of visual perception therefore seems now to apply only to an isolated component of my sensory experience – the bare input of colours and light. But this isolated component is itself the result of theoretical analysis and is never the actual object of our conscious experience. Must I not always perceive the red and yellow colours of the tulip at some distance from me? And does not that distance necessarily imply my actively drawing upon the sense of touch as I construct an estimate of that distance as it would be experienced in the kinaesthetic sensation as I move towards it?

Again, in a passage that already appears in the first edition of the *Three Dialogues*, Philonous asks Hylas to consider the perception of a cherry:

> A *cherry*, I say, is nothing but a congeries of sensible impressions, or ideas perceived by various senses: which ideas are united into one thing (or have one name given them) by the mind; because they are observed to attend each other.[36]

Here the single, countable cherry that I perceive is really an aggregate of different inputs to different sense-modalities, and it has no intrinsic unity. It is the subject who introduces any unity it might have, and who marks that unity with the name 'cherry'. This fruit is not therefore given as an object of passive perception, but involves my active participation in moulding the ideas given in perception into a unified object.[37] Its form, one might say, is constituted by my active mind.

The appearance of these passages in the 1713 edition of the *Three Dialogues* would suggest that the development that we have postulated is not one that is alien to the original thinking of the *Three Dialogues*, and to the early philosophy in general. It is better seen as the unfolding of what was already implicit in Berkeley's thinking about perception and unity. Sense perception, for Berkeley, always involved a unifying spiritual activity that is not actually seen in the phenomenal idea.[38]

It should be noted that this unifying activity of the mind is quite different from the act of sensation that Hylas proposed in the First Dialogue, and which was subsequently rejected by Philonous. That, after all, was a separate component of perception that actively picks out a passive object. On the Two-Component View that Hylas advocated, mental activity only reaches out to meet the object and make it present to the mind. This is quite different to the activity of unification currently under discussion, for this latter actually forms and constitutes the object itself. It 'parcels out' ideas to create a single object. In the absence of this act, the object would disintegrate back into mere ideas – the amorphous deliverance of pure sense. So, the active nature of perception we are now discussing does not, as in Hylas's Two-Component View, problematize Berkeley's immaterialism, by making mind-independent physical objects thinkable. On the contrary, it affirms immaterialism by strengthening the tie of the active mind to the object perceived, rendering the very form of the object a mental activity.

Self and mind

A further consideration must also be brought to light. So far, we have been uncritically using the terms 'activity' and 'passivity' as if it is immediately obvious what they mean. Activity, in this innocent sense, means a source of change, or a force modifying a thing; while passivity characterizes that which is acted upon or modified. But when advocating the passivity of the perception thesis, Philonous was concerned to exclude activity in a narrower sense than this. He meant *conscious* activity – activity that I am aware of being the author and agent of. That is why he allowed only deliberate, volitional acts to be active.

The more inclusive understanding of activity which we have been appealing to would incorporate not just conscious mental processes, but unconscious or barely conscious ones that govern the production of the perceived object. These are not deliberately undertaken or willed. On the definition of activity that Hylas and Philonous are working with, these processes would most likely be thought of as passive precisely because they do not stem from my conscious self. I am not usually directly aware of them and do not orchestrate them. The objects that we perceive – tulips, cherries, chairs – are really the products of a unifying mental activity that occurs out of the sight of the conscious self and is not therefore active in the narrow sense of the discussion in the First Dialogue.

There is a tension here, in Berkeley's thought, between a narrow and a broad sense of mental activity. The narrow sense results from his identification of the mind with the self. In the *Principles*, Berkeley treats 'mind, spirit, soul or myself' as synonymous.[39] This will mean that all mental activity will be *my* activity, in the sense of flowing from my conscious will. But in the second broader sense of mental activity, we refer to an original power that is internal to the mind, but which we may or may not be (fully) conscious of. This kind of activity is perhaps better characterized as 'spontaneity', meaning active power that operates of its own accord. When the mind is characterized by spontaneity it becomes a more capacious individual than my conscious self, performing activities that may be undirected by my conscious will – and even unknown to it – and yet undetermined by any outside compulsion. My suggestion is that such a broader view of the mind is only properly developed in the 1734 edition of the *Three Principles* and, with greater elaboration, in *Siris*, where the strict identification of the mind with the conscious self has evidently been relaxed or even abandoned. The development of Berkeley's thought sees his concept of mind or spirit extend beyond the focus of consciousness. It is this development that means he can *openly* endorse the synthetic understanding of perception.

The coherence of Berkeley's mature view of sense perception

Let me now draw together the different perspectives of this chapter and come to an overview of Berkeley's development on sense perception and the self. I have argued that there are two claims in Berkeley's *Three Dialogues* that are potentially in tension with one another. Firstly, there is the claim that the self or soul is purely active. This active nature does not, however, sit well with the view of sense perception in the First Dialogue which treats perceiving as nothing over and above the immediate and passive content of ideas. How can a self who is purely active perceive these ideas at all? And how can it exist and be aware of itself in intervals where only the passive state of perception obtains?

We have seen that Berkeley provides for himself a solution to these problems by developing a more complex account of sense perception of which there are hints in the early philosophy – in the Notebooks and the *Essay on Vision* – but which is first properly advanced in the 1734 edition of the *Three Dialogues*. This holds that the mind actively unites the passive perceptions of different sense-modalities into the objects of experience. This view was already implied by the theory of vision in his earlier writings, as well as by his (related) approach to number. It means that the mind is spontaneously active in sense perception, collecting ideas under a concept of what they are (a tulip, a cherry, a human body, etc.). Such an active view of perception is then given emphatic expression ten years later in *Siris*. It brings certain advantages to Berkeley's overall account of the mind. Most importantly it enables us to understand how the mind can be characterized as an active nature and yet still be the subject of perceptual experience, and it makes it possible to explain why during periods when we are only perceiving there is actually no suspension of this active nature.

Of course, any account of perception must incorporate a passive ingredient as the subject is acted upon from without, and that will be true of Berkeley's account in his mature view. The active conception of spirit, while it excludes 'inertness', or lack of causal power, does not exclude passivity – the suffering of action from outside.[40] In *Siris*, Berkeley talks of passively received 'elements' being the material that is combined into units or objects.[41] The signal point, however, is that perception on this account is never reducible to a mere passive suffering of external action, because it necessarily involves a continuing unifying act of the mind itself. Passive uptake and active processing are inseparable in sense perception, and the objects perceived are produced by a continuous interplay of external divine cause and internal active subject.

6

Berkeley's conceptual dynamism

We noted in Chapter 5 that, for Berkeley, sense perception is penetrated by concepts, and we saw how the mind parcels the input of sense into different countable objects according to a conception of what is represented. This now brings us to the question of what exactly a concept is for Berkeley. Answering this question is not straightforward because Berkeley did not use the term 'concept' or any equivalent. So, there is no obvious place in his writings where he discusses what a concept consists in, let alone a place where he gives an explicit definition of concepts or conceptual thought. As a first step, we must therefore make it plain what *we* mean by the term, and how we understand conceptual thinking. Only then will we be able to investigate Berkeley's writings for evidence of what his view might be.

What is a concept?

What does it mean to say that I have a concept of 'triangle', 'the gothic novel' or of the 'oak'? Above all, it implies that I have an ability to think generally about particulars. My concept of a triangle enables me to think not just about a single particular instance of the shape, but to think about many different instances of it, all at one and the same time – I am able to think about triangles in general. My having a concept of a triangle also enables me, in normal circumstances, to distinguish shapes that are not triangular from ones that are.

If a concept enables us to think generally, and to recognize particulars that do or do not fall under the concept, it also brings with it a kind of unity. To have a concept is to unify particulars and treat them all as sharing in some common feature or features that other particulars do not share in. Conceptual thinking involves our being aware of unity in diversity – we grasp how numerically different particulars, with differing qualities as well as qualities in common, fall under one and the same category. Thus, two different triangles, one of which is (say) isosceles and one of which is right-angled, are understood as being the same *qua* triangles.

The temptation of abstraction

Now, as Berkeley realized, it is very tempting, when explaining conceptual thought, to postulate abstract content in the mind. Such content, we naturally feel, has the potential to explain both the generality *and* the unity of conceptual thought. Abstraction offers generality because it excludes the concrete and particular; it also offers unity because the abstract prototype can remain single and unchanging in its manifold applications. This seemed obvious to Locke who posited a process of abstraction to explain the derivation of conceptual thought from the data of sensation and reflection. A parallel view is offered by Descartes and his followers. While the Cartesians did not, of course, hold that there was a *process* of abstraction from sensory particulars, they did conceive their perceptions of the pure intellect as abstract in the sense of lacking particular features.[1]

Berkeley was fundamentally opposed to explaining concepts by abstract ideas. Two kinds of abstract ideas were explicitly characterized as the targets of his critique. The first kind were simple ideas arrived at by singling out specific qualities from others, as in the case when I attempt to conceive of red without extension. This kind of abstraction would bring universality through simplicity.[2] While a given patch of burgundy red with its particular shape and extension is exceptional and peculiar, burgundy red alone – when separated from shape and extension – becomes a universal colour hue. Berkeley's objection to such simple abstract ideas is *not* that there is a formal contradiction involved, but that the simple abstract idea is not a possible object of the mind. Our mental powers are not able to achieve the separation of a given shade of red from the quality of extension. This reflects Berkeley's rejection of Lockean simple ideas that was discussed in Chapter 3. Berkeley departs from the key thesis of Locke's concept empiricism that analyses the blended sensory given into discrete *simples* which can then be recombined in the imagination, allowing us to 'compound' new complex ideas.[3]

Secondly, there are general ideas that are abstract by virtue of lacking *any* particularity – ideas of triangularity, humanity, motion or of colour that is no longer a burgundy red, say, but colour per se.[4] His principal argument against these general ideas is that they contain contradictory predicates and therefore cannot stand before the mind as the objects of thought, nor can they even exist. In the famous case of the abstract idea of a triangle, Berkeley treats Locke as exposing the internal contradictions of his own doctrine when he states that such an idea 'must be neither oblique nor rectangle, neither equilateral, equicrural, nor scalenon, but all and none of these at once. In effect, it is something imperfect that cannot exist'.[5]

Berkeley not only denied abstract ideas as possible objects of thought, he also treated abstractionist explanations of concepts as the source of a range of philosophical ills. One undesirable result of seeking abstract ideas is that we are led away from context and relations, as when we assume there is an abstract idea of space or goodness, and fail to appreciate how those words apply only to relations between particular things.[6] In addition, it is the doctrine of abstraction that has fostered an erroneous belief in matter – a putative entity which draws on the impossible abstract idea of existence, separated from perception.[7] More generally, the talk of abstractions constitutes one way in which philosophers have thrown up 'a learned dust' and perpetuated dispute.[8] So Berkeley's account of conceptual thought will involve no abstract mental contents.

Concepts – formation and possession

To understand Berkeley's alternative to abstractionist accounts of conceptual competence, we must now introduce a further distinction in our consideration of concepts: we must distinguish between the question of *acquisition* and the question of *possession* of concepts. The question of how we acquire a concept, is the one of how a child – or anyone innocent of the concept – can first form it in her mind. The question of the possession, on the other hand, concerns how we maintain a concept, once acquired. Possession of a concept is our continuing knowledge of what the word identified with the concept means.

All theories of concept acquisition will surely involve some degree of activity on our part. Certainly, this is true of the two principal accounts that Berkeley would have been acquainted with when reading Locke and Descartes. For Locke, we acquire a concept by forming an abstract idea – extracting from the data of experience a universal. On seeing, for example, various objects of a white colour, such as snow, chalk and milk, we are able to isolate the universal of whiteness, separating it from the diverse particular things which it inheres in.[9] Locke never tells us exactly how the abstract skeleton is removed from the garment of sense, so to speak, and only makes a broad appeal to a 'power' of abstraction. But he does stress that abstraction is a process which children must learn and which animal minds are unable to perform at all.[10] Concept formation is thus an exertion of the human mind, to which Locke gives the name 'abstracting', and which he includes among our core mental operations.[11]

Equally, Descartes's innatist theory involves an active process of concept formation. It is true that the innate idea is drawn from a stock of inborn ideas within the mind. But for the mind to possess the concepts of God, space, number and so on, it must turn towards these ideas within itself, which, at best, have been intimated to it in sense experience. Concept formation is therefore again an active process, and Descartes clearly thinks that many people – including some philosophers – are not able to perform the inward turn that enables us to arrive at concepts of the pure intellect. The activity of concept formation here, though it is certainly different to the abstractionist accounts, is no less an active operation of the mind.

If we now ask what it takes to *possess and maintain* a concept for Locke and Descartes then they both provide an answer that no longer needs appeal to any formative mental activity. On the contrary, a concept, once established, is perceived by the mind standing before it as an idea. Locke tells us quite clearly that an idea is 'whatsoever the Mind perceives in it self',[12] and the abstract ideas associated with a general thought can be no exception. We behold our abstract ideas. Our possession of a concept, and our application of it, is grounded in a perception of a single unchanging idea.

Descartes, too, uses the language of perception to explain our understanding and possession of concepts. The Cartesian account has us perceiving ideas that are immediately present to the mind's eye. We are, of course, setting aside for the moment the radical differences between the accounts of these two thinkers – in particular we are ignoring the fact that the Cartesian account involves the vision of the intellect (*purus intellectus*) which Locke has no place for. The possession of a concept, in their otherwise divergent theories, is an affair of inward perception in which the mind passively takes in representational content, just as the mind passively sees or hears in sense perception. Malebranche, too, though he eschews both abstraction and innatism in his account of our conceptual capacity, still affirms the static perceptual model of concept possession. We *see* ideas in God.

So, on two accounts that Berkeley would have been well-acquainted with, the perception of a peculiar object by the mind was the key to our possession of a concept. While concept formation may have been a process or task performed by the mind, concept possession was a passive affair, in which an established mental representation continues to stand before the perceiving mind.

Berkeley's dynamic approach to concept possession

Berkeley's radical break with these models is to treat conceptual competence as a continuing activity of the mind. To have and sustain a concept is to be engaged in *doing* something, and not merely to perceive something. A concept is more like a mental skill than an inward representation. To possess a concept is to have mastered a technique, not to have stored in the memory an abstract item.

It is true that, for Berkeley, there is a necessary perceptual element in concept possession. The skill we exhibit when we understand or deploy a concept makes active use of concrete imagery. When one comprehends what a triangle is, for example, one has before the mind a perception of a particular triangle, with a particular set of angles and sides. But that concrete triangle maintains its generality by its being used to represent other concrete triangles. The class of those other triangles is circumscribed by how the concrete triangle before the mind is employed.

It is also true that language (composed of signs that are shapes and sounds) is used to provide a stable framework for the use of concepts both intersubjectively, and within the mind of the individual. General names, with conventional signification, have their meaning fixed and determined by the 'necessary' circumscriptions of shared definition.[13] Nevertheless, the possession and understanding of the general concept in the mind of the individual is constituted by the active deployment of concrete imagery in thinking. One example of this is the way a particular shape or line is used in a demonstration to stand for other shapes or lines:

> An idea, which considered in itself is particular, becomes general, by being made to represent or stand for all other particular ideas of the same sort. To make this plain by an example, suppose a geometrician in demonstrating the method, of cutting a line in two equal parts. He draws, for instance, a black line of an inch in length, this which in itself is a particular line is nevertheless with regard to its signification general, since as it is there used, it represents all particular lines whatsoever.[14]

It is this active or dynamic nature of concept possession, revealed here in the geometrical demonstration undertaken, that makes Berkeley's account importantly different to other approaches to conceptual competence in his time. Berkeley's dynamic approach to concepts diverges from the static, quasi-visual, models of concept possession popular among his early modern predecessors and contemporaries.[15]

One important implication of his dynamic account is that the intellect is not a purely passive faculty. Our intellectual abilities are not grounded solely in a passive recognition of the nature of concepts. I cannot simply examine an inert mental representation, however complex, in order to understand what a triangle is, or what a gothic novel is, or what an oak tree is. Rather, these general categories consist in my deploying particular ideas of sense, making them represent and stand for other ideas of sense. In the case of the triangle I use a particular triangle, in my mind, or in a diagram before me, to represent other particular triangles. It is my competent use of the triangle in this representative role that constitutes my understanding of the *concept* triangle. This understanding is not equivalent to some peculiar representation, or *Vorstellung*, in which certain particular features have been 'blanched out'. Intellectual understanding is our ability to do things with our ideas, and it is hard to see how, on Berkeley's view, it could easily be separated from action and will.

Hume's misinterpretation of Berkeley

So far, we have spoken broadly of the role of *activity* in concept possession. To understand the kind of activity involved in Berkeley's account, it will be helpful to compare it to the closely related theory of general thought offered by David Hume. Hume admired Berkeley's critique of abstract ideas, lavishing it with praise in the *Treatise*:

> A very material question has been started concerning *abstract* or general ideas, *whether they be general or particular in the mind's conception of them.* A great philosopher has disputed the receiv'd opinion in this particular, and has asserted, that all *general* ideas are nothing but particular ones, annexed to a certain term, which gives them a more extensive signification, and makes them recall upon occasion other individuals, which are similar to them. …
> I look upon this to be one of the greatest and most valuable discoveries that has been made of late years in the republic of letters.[16]

Hume sought to incorporate Berkeley's insight (as he understood it), into his own radical empiricist position. He accepted Berkeley's negative thesis, that an abstract idea is something that cannot be present to the mind. He then offered a positive associationist account of how we can think generally in the absence of abstract ideas. While it is clear from the passage just quoted that Hume thought his account of general thought was still faithful to Berkeley, in fact it was significantly different. Indeed, the difference between the two thinkers is already signalled in Hume's claim that a 'term' or word enables a particular idea to 'recall upon occasion other individuals'. Hume's account supposes an attractive or 'associative' force acting between ideas (for words are sensory ideas, or perceptions, too). This is something that plays no discernible role in Berkeley's account of conceptual competence.

I will expand on this crucial point of difference in a moment, but first let me stress the points of similarity between the two authors. Both deny the existence of abstract or intrinsically general ideas. They agree that only particular, concrete ideas can come before the mind. They therefore also agree that only such particular mental content is available to us in any philosophical explanation of the generality of thought. Most importantly, though, both authors assert that a particular idea is made general by its role in a *temporally extended* activity. In the absence of abstract ideas, they both have a particular idea acquiring generality by being part of an unfolding process. They embrace what we might call the 'temporalization' of generality.

It is in their understanding of the nature of this temporal process that the difference between the two philosophers emerges. For Hume, the process in question is one that happens within us, in a mysterious way, guided by the non-conscious springs of human nature. Hume argues that, having experienced a sign referring to a variety of particular ideas, we 'acquire a custom' and 'the hearing of that name revives the idea of one of these objects, and makes the imagination conceive it with all its particular circumstances and proportions'.[17] The word also revives a host of other particular ideas to which it has associative connections – the 'revival set' as Don Garrett usefully terms them.[18] Although we do not need to survey all the members of the revival set, and we are happy to 'abridge' their production in us, we still feel their potential, and it is the presence of this potential that confers on a particular idea its general significance.[19] Thus when an image of a concrete triangle comes to my mind on hearing the word 'triangle', this idea is ready to call into my mind a chain of other particular ideas of triangles. It is this fact of association that enables me to talk and think about triangles in general, rather than only about the single triangle that I actually entertain.

In Hume's account the conscious 'I' has a passive role. It does not carry out or determine the associations. Instead members of the revival set 'well-up' from within the mind in a way that is not in the least perspicuous to us. Berkeley's account is quite different in this respect. For Berkeley, the process in question is an intentional and conscious one that I, myself conduct. It is not something that happens out of my sight in the recesses of the soul; it is rather my own 'consideration' that endows particular ideas with general significance.

This difference comes out most clearly in Hume's and Berkeley's consideration of the general ideas of geometry. It was vital, of course, for these two philosophers to give an adequate account of the demonstrative science of geometry. Any opponent of abstraction had to explain how a geometrical demonstration using a particular idea – an isosceles triangle in Berkeley's example – could give rise to a conclusion about triangles in general. How can our conclusions apply beyond the specific triangle that is present to our thoughts, or drawn on a piece of paper before us? For Berkeley, this was possible because in my demonstration I refer only to certain features of the particular triangle and overlook others:

> Though the idea I have in view whilst I make the demonstration, be, for instance, that of an isosceles rectangular triangle, whose sides are of a determinate length, I may nevertheless be certain it extends to all other rectilinear triangles, of what sort or bigness soever. And that, because neither the right angle, nor the equality, nor the determinate length of the sides, are at all concerned in the demonstration.[20]

It is by omitting any reference to the particular characteristics of an isosceles triangle that my demonstration is able to inform us of a truth about all triangles. This point is reinforced in an addition to this passage in the second edition of the *Principles* where Berkeley emphasises how 'a man may consider a figure merely as triangular, without attending to the particular qualities of the angles, or relations of the sides'.[21] The term 'consider' should – here as elsewhere – be understood as an active ability of selective attention.[22]

Hume, in contrast, treats the generality of the individual triangle in geometrical demonstration to arise from the habit of association

> after the mind has produc'd an individual idea, upon which we reason, the attendant custom, reviv'd by the general or abstract term, readily suggests any other individual.[23]

So, in Hume's account, in addition to the isosceles, right-angled triangle before my mind, ideas of other particular triangles – called up by their association with the word – press in on my consciousness, making their presence felt.

Now comes the crucial step in Hume's explanation of general thought: if I allow the peculiarities of the isosceles triangle (say, its two equal sides, or its right angle) to influence my consideration of triangles in general and thereby to restrict the scope of my proof, then other particular non-isosceles triangles will pop into my consciousness to remind me of the true breadth of the generalization I am seeking to make. Hume writes,

> Other triangles which we overlook'd at first, immediately crowd in upon us, and make us perceive the falsehood of this proposition, tho' it be true with relation to that idea, which we had form'd.[24]

At this point Hume's mysterious associative power shows real intelligence. It is able to correct my thinking and widen the scope of my proof, by summoning up well-chosen counter-examples in my imagination. It is no wonder that Hume describes this intelligent influence of association as 'a kind of magical faculty in the soul', and as 'inexplicable by the utmost efforts of human understanding'.[25] While for Berkeley the generality of conceptual thinking is led by the active conscious self, for Hume it is the result of a shadowy intelligence that acts on our consciousness from within the depths of 'human nature'.

Language, universals and nominalism

To understand Berkeley's account of conceptual thought in the introduction to the *Principles* we must also be clear about the role of language. He makes many references to language, and signs are certainly a vital ingredient in Berkeley's account of concepts in helping to fix meaning for inter- and intrasubjective use, as already indicated. But is language essential? One way of approaching this question about the role of signs in his account of concepts is to ask the further question: was Berkeley a nominalist?

Now, the term 'nominalism' is ambiguous between two separate senses that are commonly given to the term. In one meaning, nominalism is the ontological claim that everything in the world is particular. There are no general or universal entities. A second meaning of nominalism concerns the role of language in cognition. This meaning is truer to the etymology of the term (*nomen* meaning 'name' in Latin), and it says that universals are founded on words. It is the unique property of signs that they allow us to think generally, or to have universals at our command. Without signs, general or conceptual thought would be impossible.

These ontological and cognitive meanings of the term 'nominalism' are, of course, closely related, and they usually play a complementary role. If one holds that there are no universal entities in nature, then it is natural to argue that it is language – founded on human convention – which brings cognition of universals into the world. In the context of Berkeley's philosophy, however, we find that the two doctrines that go under the name 'nominalism' may be separated from one another. Berkeley is certainly a nominalist on the first, ontological, meaning of the term, at least in the early phase of his philosophy. But it is much less clear that he is signed up to nominalism in the second sense, as a doctrine about the role of language in cognition. While he clearly thinks that language is a significant aid in enabling us to think generally, it is not clear that, at any time in his career, he takes the use of words to be a necessary condition for general thought.

To appreciate how Berkeley approved of ontological nominalism, but not cognitive nominalism, we may compare him with Hobbes, who offered a trenchant defence of nominalism in both these senses. Indeed, Hobbes asserts the two doctrines within a single sentence:

> There being nothing in the world Universall but Names; for the things named, are every one of them Individuall and Singular.[26]

Hobbes argues that someone 'who hath no use of Speech at all' might recognize that the three angles of a particular triangle are equal to two right angles. But this person, lacking language, will not be able to extend this knowledge to other triangles. However, on gaining the use of language – including the word 'triangle' – the person in question may then recognize that the proof concerning one particular triangle has a universal significance. He 'will boldly conclude Universally, that such equality of angles is in all triangles whatsoever; and register his invention in these generall termes, *Every triangle hath its three angles equall to two right angles*.'[27] Thus, for Hobbes, it is the term 'triangle' that makes possible general thought about this class of shape, and thus makes universal proofs about triangles accessible.

Berkeley may seem to agree with Hobbes that it is language that lends generality to our thought. In the absence of abstract ideas, it may look as if words enable us to refer to classes of things, and thus to gain a foothold in conceptual thought. Indeed, we find Berkeley affirming, in reference to a geometrical proof, that the 'name *line* which taken absolutely is particular, by being a sign is made general'.[28] But here we come to the crucial difference between Hobbes and Berkeley. While for Hobbes there is no general thought, let alone universal geometrical proof, in the absence of linguistic names, for Berkeley thought can achieve generality prior to language, and language only *fixes* and *facilitates* the generality of thought. Berkeley writes, in the same section that we have just quoted from, that a geometrician is able to use a specific diagram in a general way prior to the use of the term 'line':

> He draws, for instance, a black line of an inch in length, this which in itself is a particular line is nevertheless with regard to its signification general, since as it is there used, it represents all particular lines whatsoever; for that what is demonstrated of it, is demonstrated of all lines or, in other words, of a line in general.[29]

For Berkeley, it is the picture of 'a black line of an inch in length' that acquires generality, and the general term 'line' is dependent on the general *use* of this particular image in the demonstration.[30] The primal act that bestows generality on a particular idea is not one that arises when a linguistic name is attached to an idea, but rather it pertains to the idea as it is employed in the mind of the individual thinker.

> An idea, which considered in itself is particular, becomes general, by being made to represent or stand for all other particular ideas of the same sort.[31]

It is how we actively deploy a particular idea, giving it a hierarchical relation to other similar ideas, and thus enabling it to stand in for them and represent them, that allows us to think generally. The name (*nomen*) is then brought in to fix this active use of a particular idea. It does not itself bestow upon the idea generality, for the idea has already been invested with general significance prior to the use of the linguistic sign. While for Hobbes it is the term 'triangle' that is properly universal, for Berkeley it is the particular image of a triangle that has a general, or universal, signification.

> Thus when I demonstrate any proposition concerning triangles, it is to be supposed that I have in view the universal idea of a triangle; which ought not to be understood as if I could frame an idea of a triangle which was neither equilateral nor scalenon nor equicrural. But only that the particular triangle I consider, whether of this or that sort it matters not, doth equally stand for and represent all rectilinear triangles whatsoever, and is in that sense *universal*.[32]

The important distinction between Berkeley's active mentalism and Hobbes's nominalism is reinforced in the second edition of the *Principles* published in 1734. It is our 'consideration' of a particular triangle, he argues, that bestows on it universality:

A man may consider a figure merely as triangular, without attending to the particular qualities of the angles, or relations of the sides.[33]

This last statement might sound like a *volte-face* and an outright admission of an abstract idea of triangularity. But this impression arises from our tacitly assuming that 'consider' means something like 'perceive', or 'view'. If, however, we treat 'consider' in a strong, active sense, we find that this statement is an extension of the earlier view.[34] It does not say that there can be an abstract image before the mind, but rather that while mental content must always be particular, and possessed of the different particular qualities that inevitably fall together (e.g. colour *and* extension), thought is more free. The generality of thought arises in the way we actively and selectively attend to the idea in question – the way we take it and 'consider' it in relation to other ideas.

Concepts as 'knowing how'

For Berkeley, to maintain and possess a concept is to be doing something. Conceptual ability is not contained in a perception, but in the exercise of what might be described as a mental *skill*. The intellectual sphere has become, for him, a peculiar kind of doing. Berkeley would join with Gilbert Ryle in rejecting the 'intellectualist legend' or the doctrine that 'defines intelligence in terms of the apprehension of truths, instead of the apprehension of truths in terms of intelligence'.[35]

Intellectual knowledge is made possible by our possession of concepts. But possession of concepts, on Berkeley's account, is not to be thought of as a 'knowing that' so much as a 'knowing how'. I have a conceptual grasp of what a line is because I can employ a concrete line as the sign for an indefinite class of other lines. I know how to use the concrete line – without taking any cognisance of, say, its particular length or colour – in a variety of proofs with lines, such as bisecting them into two equal parts, rotating them round an axis, adding one line to another and so on. The intellectualist legend would demand that a 'knowing that' underlie all these competences – to which Berkeley, like Ryle, would ask: Why? Why do we need a peculiar apprehension of an abstract idea of a line to explain the general significance we give to a particular line? That significance, Berkeley holds, is itself grounded in rule-governed activity.

Ryle, of course, tended to physical behaviourism and focused on the activities of the physical body and its dispositions to act. Berkeley, I suggest, makes the same move in the inner sphere: to have an inner conceptual competence it is not enough to be in a state of purely intellectual vision, but rather we must employ our ideas in an intelligent and purposeful way in our thinking.

Relations: 'A germ of Kantism'

It is now time to consider the significance of one of the most important steps taken by Berkeley in his philosophical development. In the Middle Period, Berkeley added relations to his list of notions. He now explicitly denied that relations are known by idea, or gathered from a perceptual representation, and he affirmed that they are acts of the mind. This new view of relations is evident in two passages added to the 1734 edition of the *Principles*:

> We know and have a notion of relations between things or ideas, which relations are distinct from the ideas of things related, inasmuch as the latter may be perceived by us without our perceiving the former.[36]

Again,

> It is also to be remarked, that all relations including an act of the mind, we cannot so properly be said to have an idea, but rather a notion of the relations and habitudes between things.[37]

These statements place relations alongside other things known by notions, including mental acts, emotions and the mind itself. But Berkeley says little more about the wider significance of his including relations among notions. It may even look like an afterthought, as if Berkeley has just remembered that there was another item which he had meant to add to his list of notions.

It is certainly possible that Berkeley had always thought of relations as known through notions, and had just not got round to pointing it out until now. However, given the reluctance that he otherwise shows in making additions to the new editions of the *Principles* and *Dialogues*, it is more probable that these insertions mark a new realization or even a shift in his thought. Yes, previously he may have been dimly aware that this view was implicit in his philosophical position, but now he properly recognizes the importance of a non-perceptual account of relations.

Relations are essential to the account of conceptual thought that is offered in the introduction to the *Principles*. Berkeley, after all, treats our capacity to *think generally* as grounded in the use of a particular idea to represent other particular ideas. An idea that has no intrinsic general characteristics therefore acquires its generality by virtue of the relations that the mind establishes between it and other ideas. Berkeley wrote, in the first edition of the *Principles*:

> Universality, so far as I can comprehend, not consisting in the absolute, positive nature or conception of anything, but in the *relation* it bears to the particulars signified or represented by it: by virtue whereof it is that things, names, or notions, being in their own nature particular are rendered universal.[38]

The significance of the additions to the *Principles* about relations is displayed in this statement. In treating relations as notions, Berkeley now makes explicit the connection between the character of notions and his account of general thinking contained in his polemic against abstract ideas. The two parts of his thought are now shown to be inseparably bound together. If generality is constituted and made possible by our actively establishing and maintaining relations between ideas that are themselves only particular, then general thought – that is, conceptual thought – is the product of the active notions of the mind.

The change has further implications. It backs up the view of sense perception that I presented in Chapter 5, according to which there is no sensory perception without active notions. The actual content of our perceptions is thoroughly penetrated by the activities of our minds. To perceive objects, after all, is to be aware of a network of relations. For example, to see a plant, a flower or a leaf *as* a plant, a flower or a leaf implies a relation of the particulars now perceived to other particulars – other plants, flowers or leaves – previously perceived. Or, if we turn to Berkeley's theory of vision, our anticipation of relations between *visibilia* and *tangibilia* enable us to see things in a certain situation, at a certain distance from us or having a certain size.

The newly presented view of relations that is introduced in 1734, then, involves two fundamental and far-reaching philosophical developments.

Firstly, it unites Berkeley's anti-abstractionism with his doctrine of notions in one dynamic theory of what it is to have a concept. If relations are acts of the mind, then conceptual competence must be constituted by these acts of mind. It is not enough to perceive ideas before the mind's eye. Fraser was right to spot 'a germ of Kantism' here.[39] Secondly, as set out in Chapter 5, it makes a purely passive account of sensory perception no longer viable. All deliverances of sense will be penetrated by the relations that the mind actively introduces between ideas. Berkeley has come to the view – once again associated with Kant – that any sensory datum is shot-through with the active judgements of the mind. To put this in another way, sense now possesses a conceptual structure.

Berkeley's dualism again

We are now in a position to see how Berkeley's account of conceptual thinking involves both sides of his ontological dualism. Ideas are the concrete images that we have before the mind when we think generally. They are all derived from sense perception, for, as Berkeley established early on, by idea is meant 'any sensible or imaginable thing'.[40] Yet, it is the way we use these images in our thinking that enables some of them to stand for classes of particular things and thereby to take on general significance. Both these constituents of Berkeley's dualism are engaged when he explains our conceptual competence. On the one hand, we have the concrete ideas of different triangles, straight lines, human individuals and so on; on the other hand, we have the active and intelligent deployment of these ideas by the mind as it uses one particular idea to represent others.

Empiricists and innatists have typically gone wrong, Berkeley would hold, in explaining our mastery of concepts by an appeal to the contemplation of a special kind of passive idea. The empiricist claim is that the special idea that corresponds to a concept is one abstracted from the *concreta* of sense. Such an abstract idea is, for Berkeley, palpably contradictory, for it would have to include inconsistent properties in order to cover all the different particulars that can fall under a concept. But innatists or 'rationalists' err too in claiming that the special idea in question is one perceived by the pure intellect. Such an object would be no less abstract and contradictory than one arrived at by a putative process of abstraction.⁴¹ Each of these two explanations of general concepts has made the mistake of confining its attention to the perceived content of ideas, and thus making a concept a special object of mental vision. Both accounts are wed to the 'new way of ideas'.

Berkeley's notions, put forward in conscious opposition to 'ideism', render his alternative, dynamic, account of intellectual understanding possible. This view is most visible in the Middle and Late Periods of Berkeley's development when he overtly includes relations among notions. Relations between particular ideas are not to be passively perceived, but are actively established by the mind in its consideration of passive perceptions. The central relation of representation, by which a particular idea takes on conceptual significance, is a relation that the mind guides and performs, rather than one it perceives.

In the Heroic Period, Berkeley's doctrine of notions not only lacked its characteristic terminology, but it had a narrow focus on the way we know ourselves and our own operations. In the Middle and Final Periods, we see the doctrine being extended to a non-perceptual understanding of conceptual thought. If sameness is the arch-relation that makes conceptual thought itself possible by enabling us to conceive unity in the diversity of particulars, then the assertion of *Siris* that 'likeness' and 'parity' are active notions of the mind becomes fully comprehensible.⁴² In this assertion, one can see how Berkeley's doctrine of notions has now merged with his anti-abstractionist account of general concepts, and notions have taken the role that abstract ideas played in the empiricist tradition – that of enabling intellectual thought.

7

A notion of goodness

The doctrine of notions does not only concern direct consciousness of one's own mind and its activities. It comes to have a much broader significance for Berkeley, grounding our knowledge of ethics, aesthetics, mathematics and theology. The list of notions in the final stage of his career, stated in *Siris*, comprises 'being, beauty, goodness, likeness, parity'.[1] This list bears a notable resemblance to the forms enumerated in Plato's *Theaetetus*,[2] which, Socrates tells us, the soul grasps 'through itself'.[3] These – in different variations – came to be called the transcendentals (*transcendentalia*) by the scholastics, who looked upon them as the primitive predicates common to all beings and the foundations of metaphysics. While Berkeley's inclusion of 'being' at the head of this list will refer to active spirit, whether in its finite or divine instances, the remaining notions here refer, inter alia, to the elements of aesthetics, ethics and mathematics.

In this chapter and Chapter 8, I shall consider the wider applications of the doctrine of notions, indicated by this list of the transcendentals in *Siris*, focusing on three kinds of direct knowledge: knowledge of moral goodness, of number, and of the divine mind. In each case we see how Berkeley, in the early Heroic Period, begins by stressing the negative part of the doctrine, resisting perceptual accounts of such knowledge that postulate either abstract or complex ideas, constructed and perceived by our minds. Berkeley's opposition to ideas constituting the fundamentals of ethics, mathematics and theism is, then, supplemented, in the Middle and Final Periods, by a more positive account of how we arrive at our understanding of these aspects of reality, drawing on the active power of our own simple natures. In this chapter, we shall begin by focusing on Berkeley's notion of goodness and on Berkeley's approach to ethics.

Ethics in Berkeley's writings

Ethics has a prominent – though largely implicit – place in Berkeley's overall philosophical project. He held that our approach to the speculative and theoretical questions of philosophy is not ethically indifferent. The system we adopt in natural philosophy will have an important influence on the wider morality in the given society. The materialist corpuscularian world view, argued Berkeley, had engrossed people's minds with corporeal objects and determined laws of motion, thus making them receptive to 'fatalism' and 'Sadducism' and to a kind of ethical egoism that looked upon public spiritedness as 'a generous folly'.[4] There can be little doubt that he hoped his own philosophy would provide a grounding for the renewal of public morality.

Despite this ethical background to his philosophy, Berkeley does not offer an extended and systematic discussion of moral philosophy anywhere in his extant works. There are indications in the Notebooks that the lost Second Part of the *Principles* was to deal with ethics alongside spirit.[5] But until the day that lost manuscript is retrieved, we must be content to examine the hitherto extant texts looking for passages or remarks that indicate Berkeley's views in the field of ethics. There are two publications that immediately stand out in this regard. One is the short discourse *Passive Obedience* (1712) which makes a series of programmatic statements on the moral law and its theological background in its early sections. However, despite the significance of these statements, the main part of *Passive Obedience* is devoted to questions belonging to the political and legal sphere and has little to say about ethics as such. Moreover, *Passive Obedience* is a work that Berkeley did not seek to publish in a new edition after 1713. This is no doubt connected with his subsequent doubts about the wisdom of passive obedience itself as a political doctrine, but it also makes it hard for us to attribute the moral philosophy in the opening passages to Berkeley in the succeeding years of his development. The second publication is the apologetical *Alciphron* (1732), or more precisely its first three dialogues. While the ethical discussion here is informative of what Berkeley opposed, it is of less importance as a positive source for his own ethics. The polemical attacks often fall into *ad hominem* satire and the discussion is presented for a broad readership, with Berkeley clearly intending to diminish the prestige in the eye of the public of the authors he disapproves of.

Given these limitations, it pays to look beyond these two texts to other places in Berkeley's *oeuvre* where revealing comments on ethics and ethical concepts are made: these include entries in the Notebooks, often accompanied by 'Mo' in the margin; certain sections of the *Principles* and the *Three Dialogues*; essays he contributed to the *Guardian* and, most importantly, the latter part of Berkeley's final philosophical work, *Siris*. I believe these different sources – when studied alongside *Passive Obedience* and *Alciphron* – allow us to discern an underlying and consistent view of moral knowledge and, most importantly, an overall conception of the nature of the good.

Goodness and virtue in the Heroic Period

In the Notebooks, Berkeley is already clearly opposed to reconciling moral knowledge with the 'new way of ideas', rejecting any account of moral concepts as a special species of idea. 'We have no Ideas of vertues and vices, no Ideas of Moral Actions,' he writes, and he takes 'the morality [to] consist in the Volition chiefly'.[6] Ideas as inactive presentations fail to capture the active part of our beings, and it is that part of us that is engaged in moral thought and action.[7] It is Locke's mistake to understand moral experience in terms of ideas and then to project a demonstrative science of morality.[8] Such an approach misconstrues the essence of ethics, and it is no wonder that Locke found his demonstrative science to be an unsurmountable challenge. Morality is irreducibly active and it must be related directly to the will, and the modes of willing that will later be described as notions.

If the Notebooks generally reject ideas of morality, the *Principles* §100 more narrowly oppose abstract ideas of moral good.

> What it is for a man to be happy, or an object good, everyone may think he knows. But to frame an abstract idea of happiness, prescinded from all particular pleasure, or of goodness, from everything that is good, this is what few can pretend to. So likewise, a man may be just and virtuous, without having precise [that is, abstract] ideas of *justice* and *virtue*. The opinion that those and the like words stand for general notions abstracted from all particular persons and actions, seems to have rendered morality

difficult, and the study thereof of less use to mankind. And in effect, the doctrine of abstraction has not a little contributed towards spoiling the most useful parts of knowledge. (Emphasis in the original)

Our pursuit of an abstract representation of goodness or justice has ended up making these qualities obscure to us, for they are not essences that can be passively contemplated, they are active dispositions exhibited in a multitude of circumstances. This amounts to the denial that there is any sharp distinction between a proper understanding of what goodness is, and the practice of good action. To appreciate the good, one must have experience of *being* good, and a purely theoretical grasp of ethics is thus excluded.

The anti-abstractionist argument of the *Principles* is then backed up by a complementary claim, to be found in the *Three Dialogues* three years later, consistent with the view of the Notebooks mentioned earlier, that ethical concepts have nothing in common with the perceptual qualities which are represented by ideas. As we have seen the term 'idea', in accord with its root meaning, is equivalent to a sensory image for Berkeley. Notions, on the other hand, are not derived from sense. Berkeley already suggests in the first edition of the *Three Dialogues* of 1713 that virtue, along with reason and God, may be knowable by the pure intellect when that faculty is properly understood.[9] As in the Notebooks, it can be seen that Berkeley has begun to make room for the peculiar non-sensory knowledge of virtue that he later refers to with the term 'notion'.[10]

In *Passive Obedience*, published the year before the *Three Dialogues*, the essentially active character of goodness is sharply distinguished from the internal feelings of 'tenderness and benevolence of temper'. While such sentiments may help motivate moral behaviour, they cannot be the foundation of morality. Berkeley reminds us – like Kant after him – that even benevolent feelings must be restrained and judiciously governed 'otherwise they may possibly betray us into as great enormities, as any other unbridled lust'. The sentiments of 'tenderness and benevolence of temper' hold the peculiar danger for the moral agent of being 'more plausible, and apt to dazzle and corrupt the mind with the appearance of goodness and generosity'.[11] Berkeley rejects sensual understanding of the good, however benign in appearance.

Ethics in the Middle and Final Periods

The dynamic and thoroughly non-sensory model of ethical knowledge that is sketched in the Heroic Period is extended, in the Middle Period, in Berkeley's critique of moral sense theory that he presents in *Alciphron*. Berkeley looks askance at talk of 'the abstracted delight of the mind, the enjoyments of an interior moral sense, *to kalon*'. Goodness, justice and virtue are not known by any kind of perceptual representation – however delicate and elevated it purports to be. These moral qualities cannot stand before the mind and be appreciated in contemplation. Instead, they are known through our actions, and through our empathetic understanding of the actions of others.[12]

Berkeley's opposition to moral sense theory is of a piece with his principled rejection of Locke's 'internal sense' of reflection, a rejection that is trenchantly expressed in his Notebooks when, as we saw in Chapter 3, he declared that 'the grand Mistake is that we think we have Ideas of the Operations of our Minds'.[13] We should not forget that Shaftesbury, the immediate target of the critique in the Third Dialogue of *Alciphron*, had extended Locke's internal sense when developing his doctrine of 'reflected sense', by which he accounted for aesthetic and moral experience.[14] Shaftesbury talks of 'an inward eye' which 'distinguishes and sees the fair and shapely, the amiable and admirable, apart from the deformed, the foul, the odious or the despicable' as it surveys our inner affections and motives.[15]

Shaftesbury's moral sense theory had asserted a strong analogy between moral and aesthetic experience. Berkeley detects in this a denial of the essentially active nature of goodness and a kind of self-enrapt contemplation. Virtue is a principle of action, Berkeley never tires of insisting, and one example he gives is the religious virtue of faith. This is not an 'indolent perception', but 'an operative persuasion of mind, which ever worketh some suitable action, disposition, or emotion in those who have it', he writes.[16] Virtue and goodness are active powers, operating whether in our own minds and thoughts or in the outside world. But operations are not known by idea, they are known through being performed by the mind.

Berkeley's discussion of the religious virtue of faith, just mentioned, gives us some insight into the relation between sentiments and virtue. By characterizing virtue as 'an operative persuasion of mind, which ever worketh some suitable action, disposition, or emotion in those who have it', he would seem to determine the relation between moral good on the one hand, and the emotion or sentiment on the other. Knowledge of goodness is 'an operative persuasion of mind' that precedes and gives rise to the appropriate feelings and sentiments. The tenderness that is the product of the operative persuasion of virtue will be conducive of good behaviour, unlike the tenderness which results from immoral or amoral sources, such as cowardice or indulgence. In this way, Berkeley's rejection of sentimentalist theory does not involve a rejection of the relevance of sentiments altogether, it only asks that they be 'restrained and judiciously governed' as he put it in *Passive Obedience*, by the prior active power of moral goodness.

In *Siris*, the claims about the good are now put into the context of a dynamic understanding of the Platonic forms. Berkeley writes: 'In Plato's style, the term *idea* doth not merely signify an inert inactive object of the understanding, but is used as synonymous with αἴτιον and ἀρχή, cause and principle'.[17] And in the same section he says that virtue, goodness and other such moral concepts are originally existent in the soul of man 'as light to enlighten, and as a guide to govern'. Berkeley's Platonism is an expression of his enduring view that moral understanding is a power that governs our spiritual activities and is not an object of mental vision or passive contemplation. To know the good is to be actively guided by it in one's conduct – it is not to have achieved special theoretical insight or an abstract representation.

Does Berkeley have a utilitarian conception of moral good?

At this point we might consider a notable line of interpretation of Berkeley's ethics according to which he offers us a utilitarian account of goodness and moral duty. This interpretation finds most support in *Passive Obedience*,[18] and it is inspired, above all, by Berkeley's frequent assertion in this work that morality and the moral law promote 'the well-being of mankind'. Samuel Rickless and Stephen Darwall have described the 'decision procedure' proposed by Berkeley for determining which action we should pursue as 'rule-utilitarian'.[19] David

Berman, taking a similar line, has treated Berkeley as a 'strong rule-utilitarian', with a notion of the moral law that allows no extenuation or exception.[20]

How are we to make sense of the exceptionless status of moral law? Berman and Rickless both understand Berkeley's recommendation of unconditional adherence to the law of passive obedience as utilitarian in motivation, despite his open recognition that this adherence may cause, in certain situations, significant and avoidable suffering and evil. They hold that it is the general tendency of the law of passive obedience in preventing the miseries of anarchy and civil strife that, for Berkeley, means loyalty to the supreme civil power ought to be observed even when rebellion presents us with an opportunity to end tyranny and misery and thus relieve 'great sufferings and misfortunates ... to very many good men'.

The rule-utilitarian interpretation is open to challenge even when it is confined to a reading of Berkeley's justification of political loyalty in *Passive Obedience*. One problem is that utilitarianism is actually rather hard to equate with the perfectly rigid attachment to the moral law that Berkeley enjoins. Mill, perhaps the most prominent rule-utilitarian, saw that the very principle of utility made it necessary to recognize exceptions were the extent and certainty of suffering caused by obeying the moral law was overwhelming, or where – to use Berkeley's words – 'great sufferings and misfortunates ... to very many good men' will occur. A moral rule can never be absolute because these exceptions must always be made, argued Mill, if we are to uphold the happiness principle that recommends the rule in the first place. We should not become slaves to our rules, Mill wrote, like the doctor 'who prefers that his patients should die by rule rather than recover contrary to it'.[21]

A more important problem with the utilitarian reading, however, is the sense of 'well-being' appealed to in Berkeley's discussion. His use of the term should not to be understood in terms of a calculation of pleasure and pain, or, indeed, in terms of a surplus of worldly contentment over suffering.[22] He means 'well-being' in a fundamentally theological sense with reference to one's 'eternal interest', and therefore it necessarily includes the perspective of a lasting future state.[23] Indeed, Berkeley openly criticizes the equation of pleasure with moral good. While he allows that we may naturally begin by following the dictates of 'sensible pleasure', we grow to discover 'goods' of 'too refined a nature', or 'far too excellent', to affect the senses.[24] The hedonistic pleasures focused upon by Bentham and his followers are, for Berkeley, 'momentary enjoyments', not true goods, and they fail to speak to the real nature of our 'well-being' which is constituted by lasting, other-worldly, pleasure. Whether or not we agree with him on this point, we must recognize that our current sensory experience, however delectable or awful, will not in itself constitute true ethical good or evil for Berkeley as it does for the utilitarians.[25]

The content of Berkeley's notion of goodness

Berkeley claims, throughout his career, that goodness is not to be known as a peculiar abstract object that might stand before the mind, as some interpretations of Platonic *Ideas* have held. Nor, again, is the good an object of an internal moral sense that may be cultivated in a kind of moral aestheticism. Good is simply not reducible to any perceptual experience, however satisfying, rich or transporting. Instead, as the different statements that we have looked at attest, good is a principle of spiritual activity, it is a way of acting and conducting oneself, in accordance with the law, 'suggested and inculcated by conscience'.[26]

What then characterizes this activity of goodness? Much is to be learnt from a study of Berkeley's essays in the *Guardian*, of which no. 126 is especially important. Here, Berkeley writes of a 'benevolent uniting instinct implanted in human nature', which is 'the great spring and source of moral actions', and he compares this spiritual principle with the Newtonian principle of universal attraction in the physical world.[27] Indeed, the power of gravitation is treated as a kind of external foreshadowing of the moral good. This arresting ethical analogy no doubt shows why a proper understanding of Newton's physics was so important to Berkeley, and it also indicates two distinctive facets of his conception of the good. The first of these, which we have already established in the preceding discussion, is that moral good, as an active power, is not, itself, to be discovered by perception, though its effects may be. In physics, the power of gravitation, Berkeley argued throughout his career, will not be understood if we try to grasp it by perceptual ideas. This way we may be able to trace and record what gravitation brings about – the movement or rest of different bodies – but the actuating force itself will elude us. We certainly may have ideas of, say, the movement of the oceans relative to the moon. But we can have no direct idea of the force by which the moon drags the water to herself, causing the tides. If we want to grasp this force of gravitation itself it must be taken as an operation of spirit, like the operations of our own minds, and it is known by 'notion'. Good too is such an operative force.

The second facet of the analogy with gravitational attraction gives us insight into the content of the good, revealing the kind of force or power that goodness consists in. Just as gravitational attraction is an integrating force which draws bodies together and holds them in coherent relations, so good performs a parallel role in the spiritual sphere. The force of good draws us towards one another, creating and sustaining 'communities, clubs, families, friendships, and all the various species of society'. Good is supplemented by, and indeed sometimes opposed by, the deeply rooted instinct of self-love and by the 'private passions and motions of the soul',[28] but – despite these modifications and resistances – it tends to 'model everyone to that behaviour which best suits with the common well-being'. It organizes and harmonizes us into realizing the 'good of the whole' which is 'inseparable from that of the parts'. Good is equivalent, for Berkeley, to the exercise of Christian charity and is the enactment of the golden rule 'love thy neighbour as thyself'.

In *Siris*, this analogy with gravitation is reasserted and further developed. We now learn more about the activity that constitutes goodness. It is a binding activity that 'produceth concord and union, assembles, combines, perfects, and preserves entire'.[29] As such it is associated not so much with intellect, as with the spiritual power of love.[30] Extended analogy is again made with how the attractive and cohesive forces in nature 'causeth all things to hang together',[31] and how they form 'the strongest bond and cement, which holds together all the parts of the universe'.[32] Moreover, Berkeley now clearly states the nature of goodness's opposite, evil, which flows from this conception. Evil is the source of dissension and enmity: it is that which 'scatters, divides, destroys', it is a principle of divisiveness.[33]

As a binding and unifying power, Berkeley treats the good as flowing from the primary metaphysical nature of spirit. Spirit is a simple and undivided being, with no real unity or simplicity obtaining outside it. '[The] mind', Berkeley writes in *Siris*, 'of all created beings seemeth alone indivisible, and to partake most of unity'.[34] Ideas lack intrinsic unity and are, at best, 'put together by the mind'.[35] A single city, Berkeley writes, as early as the *New Essay on Vision* of 1709, can be thought of as composed by many houses; a single house as composed of many windows and chimneys; a single window is also composed of parts and so on, with unity and oneness being relative to 'the particular draughts the mind makes of its ideas'.[36] Here Berkeley diverges from the empiricists, such as Locke and Hume, who held that there were 'simple' ideas that were the constituent parts of 'complex' ideas like the corpuscles that make up the physical things in our surroundings. This difference is visible in Berkeley's view that we understand and know the simplicity, and therefore unity, of our own spiritual selves, or minds, directly by notion.

It is the simplicity, indivisibility and natural unity of the self that is, for Berkeley the key to explaining goodness. Berkeley approvingly quotes Aristotle in *De anima* asserting, 'It is the mind that maketh each thing to be one', and Berkeley goes on to identify himself with a remark of Themistius, in paraphrase of Aristotle, according to which 'being conferreth essence, the mind, by virtue of her simplicity, conferreth simplicity upon compounded beings'.[37] It is this active power of the mind, or spirit, that enables goodness in the intersubjective sphere. Goodness seeks to impart and conserve unities in the different associations and communities that the person engages in, including, of course, the political community which is the subject of *Passive Obedience*. It is a conception of the good that therefore can be seen to shape the deeply conservative doctrine of that work.

So, goodness is an expression of this fundamental nature of spirit, or 'being'. It is the power to unify, or to impart and sustain oneness in plurality. Spirit as a simple and active substance can act to bestow oneness not only on its ideas, but also on its human environment – helping to instill cohesion by promoting fellow-feeling and nurturing community in its different forms. The anti-abstractionism of the early philosophy, and the denial of perceptual knowledge of the good, thus develops into a fuller, positive account of goodness in *Siris* as an expression of the active power that springs from the inner nature of spirit itself.

8

Number and the notion of God

In this final chapter, we will investigate how Berkeley, exploiting his doctrine of notions, explains the foundations of mathematics and the conception of God. Mathematics and theology might, at first sight, seem to be quite separate spheres, and our treatment of them together might look to be forced or artificial. The connections, however, become apparent when we recognize that an understanding of unity – or 'oneness' – is essential to both. Unity is, for Berkeley, closely related, on the one hand, to the notion of a unit and thus of number and mathematics, and on the other hand to simplicity and indivisibility, which are essential characteristics of the divine nature according to tradition.

The foundation of mathematics: unity and number

If we are to examine Berkeley's account of number we must at once distinguish between two separate issues that are not always clearly divided in the secondary literature. The first issue is how we gain an understanding of number at all. This is centred, for Berkeley at least, on the question of how we come to an understanding of oneness or unity. Such is the point of departure for mathematics and the source of our understanding of numbers, for there can only be number where there is a unit. So, the problem is equivalent to how we gain a grasp of the number one. The second question concerns arithmetic, or 'the art of counting'. This seeks an explanation of our ability to perform different operations with units, such as adding, multiplying and subtracting.

It is especially important to keep these two issues separate when studying Berkeley's approach to mathematics as he offers a different kind of response to each question. On the question of what the number one consists in, and how we ultimately understand unity (oneness), he appeals to the unifying power of the mind *qua* simple substance. On the question of how we perform arithmetic or 'the art of counting', however, Berkeley develops a formalist account, grounded in the characteristics of 'names and characters'. This gives our mathematical *notation* a non-trivial role in arithmetic and leads to his extolling the 'notation of the Arabians or Indians' as peculiarly suited to arithmetical knowledge.[1] We will be concerned in this chapter with the first question of how we grasp unity, and therefore number, at all, and we will have little to say about the formalist theory of arithmetic, which has already received insightful discussion in the literature.[2]

If the crucial question, for Berkeley, is how we can explain unity, one thing is abundantly clear – Berkeley is fundamentally opposed to any passive perception of unity. That oneness might be perceived is a view he finds in Locke's *Essay*, particularly in Locke's claim that number is a primary quality. This is to render unity a real and intrinsic property of the objects of sense, quite independent of the *activity* of mind. Berkeley treats this view as bound up with a further claim of Locke's according to which unity is a simple idea that accompanies all our sensations, and therefore any sensory experience is enough to grant us a knowledge of unity. On this view, the world comes parcelled into units,[3] and the idea of unity and number is present in sense experience as much as ideas of solidity, shape or movement.

Berkeley's voices his dissatisfaction with such a view in his Notebooks:

> Will any man say that Brutes have the ideas, unity & Existence? I believe not, yet if they are suggested by all the ways of sensation, tis strange they should want them.[4]

If Locke was right and unity was a given in sense experience, then animals would have the concept. But they do not, and we cannot explain this deficit on their part if we treat unity as an intrinsic feature of each perception or sensation. Berkeley clearly feels he is on strong ground in this regard. He thinks that animals fail to understand unity because they lack the requisite reflective and judgemental activities of the intellect. It is not clear where exactly this leaves Berkeley's view of animal minds, but the wider point of this passage from the Notebooks stands out: unity is known to us not by the sensation we share with animals, as the Lockean account would have it, but in a fundamentally different way.

It is the same point that is made more explicitly in an earlier entry in the Notebooks:

> Number not without the mind in any thing, because tis the mind by considering things as one that makes complex ideas of 'em, tis the mind combines into one, which by otherwise considering its ideas might make a score of what was but one just now.[5]

It is the mind's 'consideration' that gives things number. The mind 'combines into one', and this mental activity may make 'a score of what was but one just now'. 'Consideration' here should not be confused with perception. It is a willed, reflective activity of the mind that draws on concepts. Berkeley notes soon after:

> Number not in bodies it being the creature of the mind depending entirely on it's consideration & being more or less as the mind pleases.[6]

Number is the product ('creature') of mind. We give unity, and thus number, to things by the way we consider them and categorize them. This is a theme that Berkeley emphasizes in both the *Essay on Vision* and the *Principles*. Here, in passages that Berkeley prepared for publication, he goes further than he does in the Notebooks, leaving us in no doubt that we are dealing with conceptual knowledge.

> Number ... is nothing fixed and settled, really existing in things themselves. ... According as the mind variously combines its ideas the unit varies: and as the unit, so the number, which is only a collection of units, doth also vary. We call a window one, a chimney one, and yet a house in which there are many windows and many chimneys hath an equal right to be called one, and many houses go to the making of the city ... Whatever, therefore, the mind considers as one, that is an unit.[7]

In the *Principles* Berkeley says that number is 'so visibly relative, and dependent on men's understanding, that it is strange to think how anyone should give it an absolute existence without the mind'.[8]

This view receives its most developed treatment in the last phase of Berkeley's philosophy in *Siris*. Here we learn that unity, and the concept of number that it grounds, is an *act* of the mind.[9] Notice how this differs from saying that number is a 'creature of the mind', because that might suggest that number is the *result* of our activity rather than that activity itself. The view now expressed is that the act of numbering, and creating unity, is an inborn power of mind or spirit. Our mind *is* a unifying power, which creates the unity of experience and the unity of objects in experience.

We can now see an obvious analogy between ethics and mathematics. Just as goodness is the spiritual influence of unifying, or binding together, so number is the unification of the various deliverances of sense under a single concept. Neither goodness nor number is known by a passive perception. Both are active expressions of the simplicity and unity of spirit.

The reflections on unity and number that we have just considered might seem to make unity a purely subjective matter, something that is the result of our free will. In a sense this is true. I can, say, willingly switch from my conception of a single house to consider its many chimneys and windows, and I can also switch from thinking of many houses to considering the single city that they make up. Gottlob Frege, when commenting on these passages, recoils from Berkeley's view:

> This line of thought may easily lead us to regard number as something subjective. It looks as though the way in which number originates in us may prove the key to its essential nature. The matter would thus become one for a psychological enquiry.[10]

If there is one thing that Frege deplores it is the tendency towards psychologism in mathematics. Psychology is, after all, an empirical science that investigates contingent mental dispositions and states, and founding number on psychology will deprive mathematics of its necessity and universality. So Frege thinks something has gone very wrong.

But is Frege right to detect psychologism in Berkeley's conception of number? A case can be made for saying that Berkeley grounds number in metaphysics not psychology. Yes, the free consideration of the mind determines how we combine and parcel out ideas on different occasions. But that ability is ours because our spirit already possesses an irreducible unity. As Berkeley emphasizes in numerous places, the mind is simple and indivisible. It is this metaphysical nature of spiritual substance that is, in his view, the unchanging source of our conception of number, and of the mathematical sciences in general.

Berkeley is not, of course, saying that instead of counting apples we might count minds, and that these simple spiritual units may then provide the foundation of arithmetic. That would be absurd. Rather, it is the unity of mind which allows us to count apples by combining the tangible and visible content into countable units of fruit in the first place. Apples are, after all, mere conglomerations of sensory givens, and it is only the consideration of the mind – made public by means of the conventional sign 'apple' – that combines them into units. It is therefore not the unity of mind *qua* object of perception, but unity of mind *qua* simple, active perceiver that makes possible number and arithmetic. And this unity is most certainly not a result of empirical psychological investigation. It is uncovered and comprehended only by metaphysical reflection, not by introspective observation – a point that brings us back to the ground-note of Berkeley's philosophy of spirit: the self is not to be known by idea.

In *Siris*, this founding of unity in the active nature of spiritual substance is most explicit. And the simplicity of the finite mind is itself drawn from the nature of divine mind in a neo-Platonist spirit:

> The mind ... is individual therein resembling the divine one by participation, and imparting to other things what it self participates from above.[11]

God is thus the ultimate source of unity and it is now appropriate to turn our attention to the divine nature.

The foundation of theism: the notion of God

Berkeley's distinctive doctrine of notions, which cannot be assimilated to either empiricism or innatism, is particularly discernible when we come to his account of our conception of God. This is a subject he is at first surprisingly quiet about. While he has quite a lot to say about how we know the *existence* of God in the *Principles*, he is not nearly so forthcoming about how we conceive of God's nature. Indeed, the only explicit statements in this regard, at least in the first phase of his philosophy, are made in a passage in the *Three Dialogues*. Light is also shed on this passage by some entries in the Notebooks. Taken together with his wider views on spirit, these relatively meagre sources point to a well-defined position on how we form the concept of God that I shall now expound.

Let us begin with Berkeley's fullest statement on the formation of the conception of God, given in a speech of Philonous in the Third Dialogue:

> Taking the word *idea* in a large sense, my soul may be said to furnish me with an idea, that is, an image, or likeness of God, though indeed extremely inadequate. For all the notion I have of God, is obtained by reflecting on my own soul, heightening its powers, and removing its imperfections. I have therefore, though not an inactive idea, yet in my self some sort of an active thinking image of the Deity.[12]

Three steps are described here by which we may form a conception of God. Firstly, there is an act of self-reflection ('reflecting on my own soul'). The concept of God begins from our direct awareness of our own self, and, indeed, presupposes that we have such an awareness. No reference here is made to any other entities. Most importantly, Berkeley does not seem to presuppose any knowledge of the world of bodies or of other spirits. The whole process appears to be an internal one. It is this first step, with its implication that we ourselves will be the 'image' of God, which establishes the kind of conception involved.

The second step is then to 'heighten' our own powers. How this is done is not immediately evident – a point that I will return to below – but it is sufficiently clear from the passage that I do not attribute any new powers to God beyond what I myself have, but instead raise my own powers far above the degree in which they are found in myself.

Thirdly, Berkeley talks of 'removing imperfections'. We should notice here an important asymmetry in the language that Berkeley uses in the second and third steps. While there is no addition of powers in our conceiving of God – only a heightening of those powers we possess – there is a subtraction of something from ourselves in conceiving of God. No new nature is added, but something is removed. This perhaps makes it appropriate to talk of our conception of God, on Berkeley's view, as not just a magnified, or heightened version of our own selves, but also as a *purified* version. The purity here is one of activity. Imperfections are to be treated as passive states, as a statement by Philonous later in the *Three Dialogues* strongly suggests. God, we are told, is a being 'whom no external being can affect', and who thus 'perceives nothing by sense as we do' and is not 'affected with ... sensation at all'. Indeed, to 'feel anything by sense, is an imperfection'.[13] The point seems to be that while our human activities can never be divorced from passive states, God is an utterly 'impassive', that is, purely active, being.[14]

Berkeley against Locke's constructivism

It has been customary to read Philonous's short description in the Third Dialogue of how we form the concept of God as an empiricist account. Indeed, these brief remarks have even been assimilated to Locke's account in the *Essay*.[15] Anthony Grayling, for example, writes that here 'Berkeley is echoing Locke, who substituted this way of accounting for our knowledge of God's nature for the Cartesian claim that our knowledge of God's nature is *innate*'.[16] Grayling follows Luce and Jessop, who, when commenting on this passage in a footnote to their edition, treat it as gesturing towards standard Lockean doctrine.[17]

Berkeley's account certainly has something in common with Locke's. In both the mind actively works to form the image of God. We take the deliverances of reflection and we expand them to produce a conception of something greater than ourselves. This process can be contrasted with innatism, at least in its crudest form, in which the idea of God is not the product of 'the workmanship of the mind', but is rather to be found pre-formed within us. True, the subject has work to do even on the innatist account, for the idea of God must be brought to clear mental view. But the idea itself is not wrought by the creative power of our own mind, but rather uncovered within it. By analogy, a person may have to labour to dig up and polish a Roman coin, but it is a different kind of work from creating one in the forge.

Yet, even if Berkeley's account here has some broad similarity to the one outlined by Locke, we should not ignore a real difference. This is already signalled in the language that Berkeley uses which quite deliberately avoids echoing Locke's quasi-mechanical terminology. Indeed, I think one can detect in this passage signs of an underlying dissatisfaction with how Locke had explained our conception of God. To understand this, we must first return to the Notebooks where we find a critical comment on Locke's account of how we form a complex idea of God in his *Essay*.

At Notebooks 177, Berkeley poses to himself the following query in his spidery hand:

> G Qu: How can our idea of God be complex or compounded, when his essence is simple & uncompounded V. Locke b.2.S 35.

Although Berkeley neglects to put down the number of the chapter, he is clearly referring to the *Essay* II.xxiii.35, a section in which Locke had described how we join together ideas to form a complex idea of God. Here is the whole of Locke's section.

> For it is infinity, which, joined to our *Ideas* of Existence, Power, Knowledge, *etc.* makes that complex *Idea*, whereby we represent to our selves the best we can, the supreme Being. For though in his own Essence, (which certainly we do not know, not knowing the real Essence of a Peble, or a Fly, or of our own selves,) God be simple and uncompounded; yet, I think, I may say we have no other *Idea* of him, but a complex one of Existence, Knowledge, Power, Happiness, *etc.* infinite and eternal: which are all distinct *Ideas*, and some of them being relative, are again compounded of others; all which being, as has been shewn, originally got from *Sensation* and *Reflection*, go to make up the *Idea* or Notion we have of God. (Emphasis in the original)

Locke admits here, quite openly, that there is a problem with his own constructivist, empiricist account – and it is the very problem that Berkeley highlights in the entry in the Notebooks. If we treat our idea of God as a complex one, compounded by joining ideas from both reflection and sensation, how are we able to represent the essential simplicity and unity of God's essence? Locke while noting the problem seems content to sound a note of resignation. After all, he observes, our failure to properly represent God's essence is not in any way exceptional, since we are ignorant of the essence of the most mundane material thing (a pebble), of the lowliest living thing (a fly) and, indeed, 'of our own selves'. For Locke, the fact that we know that God exists is enough, and it is vain to seek a clear representation of what his real nature consists in.

Now, we know that Berkeley strenuously opposed Locke's sceptical stance towards real essences. In the introduction to the *Principles*, he rejected the Lockean view that our faculties are unable to 'penetrate into the inward essence and constitution of things', or, as he put later in the same book, that the 'constitution of every the meanest object is hid from our view; something there is in every drop of water, every grain of sand, which it is beyond the power of human understanding to fathom or comprehend'.[18] So we should not be surprised when Berkeley objects to this ignorance of real essence infecting the theological realm. Berkeley was not about to settle for a conception of God that leaves us unable to conceive of His simple nature, though, as we shall see, he accepted that our understanding of God's nature was far from being 'adequate'.

Another reason that Berkeley would be unhappy with Locke's account relates, of course, to the very use of 'ideas' in our conceiving of God. As he frequently insists, our access to the spiritual sphere is not 'by way of idea' at all. But this concern was probably not at issue in entry 177. Judging by entries in its proximity, Berkeley had not yet developed his principled opposition to ideas of spirit.[19] The problem is rather with the role of *compounding* in the account. In the sections preceding the one cited by Berkeley, Locke had spoken of our taking simple ideas from both reflection and sense experience in constructing a complex idea of the divine mind.[20] The complexity of this idea is striking because we not only combine ideas into a new compounded whole but, as Locke stresses, some of those constituent ideas are themselves relative and so 'are again compounded of others'.[21]

It is this layered complexity that Berkeley objects to. He wishes to do justice to God's simplicity, something that Locke concedes cannot be captured in his account of our idea of God. Apart from anything else, simplicity is what gives God's nature a *de re* unity. For Berkeley, a complex idea reflects only a provisional unity that can be dissolved whenever the mind so wishes. As we have already seen, he writes in the Notebooks, prior to this comment about God, how it is 'the mind by considering things as one that makes complex ideas of them', and he emphasizes how that unity, conferred on things by the mind, can also be withdrawn by the mind, for 'by otherwise considering its ideas [the mind] might make a score of what was but one just now'.[22] So if God is to have a real objective unity, and not just a unity relative to our considerations, then any complexity in the conception must be avoided.

These problems with complexity are no doubt the reason why Berkeley does not have Philonous talk of 'joining' together qualities and abilities in the quasi-mechanical way that Locke describes. Indeed, there is no *adding* of anything to anything else. Rather the conception of the deity has a simplicity that it borrows from our own nature that we immediately and intuitively apprehend. Philonous's description of how we arrive at the notion of God follows on from explicit statements about the indivisibility of our own selves:

> The mind, spirit or soul, is that indivisible unextended thing, which thinks, acts, and perceives. I say *indivisible*, because unextended. (Emphasis in the original)

So here, in explaining how we conceive of God, just as in his explanations of how we conceive of goodness and number, Berkeley draws on the simple nature 'of our own selves'. It is by heightening the powers of our own indivisible active being, and purifying it of the imperfection of passive affections – and thus of any susceptibility to external affection – that we gain a conception of God's simple nature. The result is a conception that is not, like Locke's, a complex construction that might be taken apart and reassembled in different ways at the mind's own pleasure. Rather it has an enduring and objective simplicity flowing from our immediate knowledge of the indivisibility of our own beings. If I am myself a monad, then I may conceive of God's monadic nature. I grasp the indivisible substance of God's nature through my own.[23]

As we have seen, Locke, with characteristic frankness, admitted that our complex idea cannot represent the simplicity of God. Yet, oddly, he still wished to stand by the theological tenet of God's simple nature. In his critique of Malebranche's vision-in-God doctrine, Locke had charged Malebranche with pretending to make sense of the simplicity of God's nature, while actually asserting its opposite – the result being a 'simplicity made up of Variety'. Locke had then openly admitted that though he, like Malebranche, believed God to be a simple being, he was ignorant of how his infinite wisdom and other perfections can be predicated of such a being.[24] Berkeley no doubt saw the distinctly uncomfortable position Locke had found himself in with regard to the nature of God. For Berkeley, it was to be diagnosed as a further symptom of Locke's denial that we have knowledge of the essence 'of our own selves'.

It is true that Berkeley recognizes that our conception of God falls far short. He tells us it is 'extremely inadequate'. But by this, he means that the conception is not 'equal' to God – *adequatio* in Latin meaning parity or equality. He is thus drawing attention to our inability to heighten our powers beyond a certain level and thus to undertake the infinite heightening of those powers that would be required by an 'adequate' conception of God. But this is hardly a defect in his account from the point of view of traditional theology. After all, an 'adequate' conception of God *should* be beyond any finite creature, and the admission of inadequacy in this respect was an expression of appropriate modesty in confrontation with the infinite divine nature. The important point, that Berkeley bids the reader to recognize, is that we can arrive at an 'image' or 'likeness' of God, however inadequate it may be. By finding in ourselves an 'active thinking image of the Deity', we can capture the simple active nature of the divine spirit. Locke's complex idea of God is, by comparison, fundamentally *unlike* Him.

The talk of treating ourselves as an image of God, and the emphasis on our soul being a 'likeness of God' reveals a further concern of Berkeley's in this discussion. He is not just seeking to explain how we conceive of God, but also to find expression for a core tenet of the Abrahamic religions, the theological doctrine of *imago Dei* which treats man as formed in God's image. Just how that doctrine should be understood had, of course, been the subject of long and continuing debate. Berkeley's answer is to make sense of *imago Dei* by treating the resemblance in question as one of a shared active spiritual nature. If, by reflecting upon, heightening and purifying our own spiritual nature we can arrive at a conception of God's nature, we also, in that very cognitive act, reveal how we are made in the image of God. Thus, Berkeley gets two things for the price of one – a conception of God and an interpretation of a significant biblical doctrine.[25]

This successful accommodation of the doctrine of *imago Dei* would be significant for Berkeley not only because it was something that Locke was little able to make sense of, but also because it established a significant contrast with the view, maintained by the Irish philosophers and theologians, Peter Browne and William King, that we have no knowledge of the real attributes of God. Browne and King are also, almost certainly, in the background of Berkeley's attack on negative theology in Alciphron dialogue four.[26]

An innate conception of God?

So, despite certain similarities, Berkeley's account of how we form a concept of God is fundamentally unlike Locke's and departs from the empiricist framework. But how does it compare with the innatist account offered by Descartes? One problem with answering this question is that Descartes's treatment of our idea of God is not entirely unambiguous, and he modified the doctrine that he had presented in the Third Meditation when he came to reply to objections, particularly to those posed by the empiricist Pierre Gassendi.

In the *Meditations*, Descartes's wording conjures up a naive version of innatist doctrine according to which the creator placed an idea of Himself in us, His creation, just as a craftsman stamps his trademark on his handiwork.[27] On such a view, it would seem that while the idea is *in* us, it is not an integral or necessary part *of* us. However, Descartes clarifies his view in reply to Gassendi, telling us that the trademark metaphor was not meant to be taken in any literal way, and it would be nonsense to look for a specific 'mark', or to ask how it is stamped on us. Rather our very thinking nature is a likeness of God. Descartes sums up his doctrine of the innate idea of God to Gassendi thus

> it is quite clear that the wholly perfect power of thought which we understand to be in God is represented by means of that less perfect faculty which we possess.[28]

So Descartes's core thesis, when stripped of metaphor, is that our essence as *res cogitans* is an image of God's nature. Reflection on our own soul is thus the path to our conception of God. Just as Berkeley talks of heightening our powers, so Descartes talks of exerting the 'power of amplifying all human perfections up to the point where they are recognised as more than human'. In addition, Descartes is ready to invoke the *imago Dei* doctrine in this respect. In the Third Meditation, he has the narrator affirm,

> I am somehow made in his image and likeness, and ... I perceive that likeness, which includes the idea of God, by the same faculty which enables me to perceive myself.[29]

Descartes would therefore be perfectly able to agree with Berkeley that my own self is a 'thinking active image' of God.

Berkeley thus stands with Descartes against his empiricist opponents in two significant and distinct respects. First, he holds with Descartes, and against Gassendi, Hobbes and Locke, that the nature of God is in principle conceivable, whatever the inevitable 'inadequacy' of that conception when it comes to the extent of his powers. Secondly, he stands with Descartes against the more specific claim of Gassendi, Hobbes and Locke that we have no knowledge of our own spiritual essence and therefore our own nature cannot constitute an image of the divine nature. In consequence of this he affirms, with Descartes, the *Imago Dei* doctrine.

Despite these similarities, it would be wrong to treat Berkeley's account as Cartesian. Most importantly, he does not share Descartes's positive conception of infinity. Berkeley's conception of God's nature builds up from an awareness of my own finite nature, whereas Descartes moves in the other direction, asserting that one can recognize one's finite nature only because one has prior access to an innate conception of infinity. While Descartes is ready to accept that the path of discovery may lead me *up* from knowledge of my imperfect self to an awareness of an infinitely perfect being, the conceptual path really leads me *down* from a positive conception of infinity to an understanding of my own imperfect and limited nature. The idea of God must have always stood in the background, even if it only became consciously accessible to me in a process of reasoning on my own nature. But Berkeley does not hold Descartes's positive, and a priori, conception of infinity. In *this* sense, if not in others, his account adopts the approach of the empiricists.

Berkeley also differs from innatist doctrine because, as we have already shown, he refuses to understand our relation to ourselves in a perceptual way, as an idea. Berkeley would baulk at the meditator's claim that I can 'perceive' my own self 'when I turn my mind's eye upon myself'. In fact, it is this kind of talk that leads us away from understanding the spiritual, and ultimately makes us look upon the mind or soul as analogous to bodily things. Descartes's innatist conception is presented in precisely the *language* of sense which, however literally it is meant, is charged with producing 'Manyfold Mistakes'.[30]

Pure intellect and the notion of God

One important question remains: what faculty do we use in understanding God in Berkeley's system? It cannot be sense which, while it provides all the evidence we have for the existence of God, fails to provide us with a conception of His spiritual nature.[31] Nor can it be the imagination, which deals with ideas derived from sense. Abstraction has, of course, been ruled out. A clue is given earlier in the *Three Dialogues*, when Berkeley briefly considers the concept of pure intellect. While he is, of course, keen to dismiss the pure intellect as an abstractive power, he holds back from ruling out the faculty of pure intellect per se. Philonous makes the following carefully worded pronouncement:

> Since I cannot frame abstract ideas at all, it is plain, I cannot frame them by the help of *pure intellect*, whatsoever faculty you understand by those words. Besides, not to inquire into the nature of pure intellect and its spiritual objects, as *virtue, reason, God*, or the like; thus much seems manifest, that sensible things are only to be perceived by sense, or represented by the imagination.[32]

It looks as if, at least at this point in his development, Berkeley was inclined to categorize our conception of God – along with virtue and reason – as a deliverance of the pure intellect. Berkeley implies that we *understand* our own natures in a radically non-sensory manner, and that we heighten and purify that understanding to arrive at a purely intellectual conception of God. As John Roberts has argued, Berkeley allowed the pure intellect to grasp our 'imperceptible substantial selves',[33] and thus also to grasp other spiritual beings such as God.

But the comment we have just quoted gives little indication of whether or not Berkeley had a developed conception of the role of pure intellect in this regard, and, what's more, the reference to pure intellect seems to sit uneasily with Berkeley's explicitly non-perceptual approach to self-knowledge. Perhaps Berkeley, seeking to put clear blue water between his own conception and the empiricist internal sense, is leaving the door open to the endorsement of pure intellect in some suitably modified form in the projected Second Part of the *Principles*. This would explain his insistence, in the *Three Dialogues*, that the task of the present discussion is 'not to inquire into the nature of pure intellect'. A cautious and non-committal consideration of the pure intellect is also to be found in *De motu*, published seven years later, where again Berkeley demarcates the sphere of pure intellect, excluding from it anything to do with space, but allowing it to be concerned 'with spiritual and inextended things, such as our minds, their states, passions, virtues and such like'.[34] The point seems to be that we know these realities from within, and that such knowledge cannot be separated from our own spiritual activity. Pure intellect was perhaps the most promising candidate among the faculties in early modern psychology that Berkeley could find to express the formation of our 'image' of God.

Goodness, number and the divine nature: the Berkeleyan approach

In this chapter and in Chapter 7, we have found that Berkeley develops a distinctive view of the fundamentals of ethics, mathematics and theism. These areas of human thought are grounded on an unmistakably metaphysical conception of the mind or spirit. This simple, active being, which we know by notion, is the source of the unifying power of the good as well as the oneness of units that make possible number. It is also the same metaphysics of spirit that gives rise to the understanding of the divine nature as resembling our own simple active natures, in keeping with the doctrine of *Imago Dei*. The affinity with innatism – particularly with the refined, reflective innatism – is seen in the explanation of our understanding of these intellectual elements by reference to our own essential nature. Yet, an affinity with empiricism is also seen in the denial of any innate *idea* of goodness, number or God. To assimilate Berkeley's thinking to one of the two sides in the famous early modern divide would be to seriously distort and diminish it. While Berkeley does give a role for perceptual knowledge by idea, his most significant metaphysical claims are developed outside the framework of the 'new way of ideas' in which the classical empiricist and innatist positions were established and elaborated. He has abandoned the crucial assumption, shared by early modern empiricist and innatist alike, that intellectual understanding involves a special form of perception, and his doctrine of notions gives theoretical expression to this highly significant break with early modern orthodoxy.

Appendix

Table 1 The development of the doctrine of notions in Berkeley's writings

Heroic period	Added in the Middle Period (from 1732)	Added in *Siris* (1744)
Self (soul, spirit)	Relations	Being
Mental operations	Faith	Likeness
Causal power		Parity
Substance		Beauty
Unity		
Virtue and goodness		
Emotions		

Notes

1 Introduction

1 As Berkeley characterizes it as early as Notebooks 19.
2 The term notion did, of course, occasionally appear earlier than 1734 in Berkeley's writings, but in a somewhat underdetermined sense meaning idea, concept or theoretical assumption. Sometimes it even took on a pejorative connotation: at PHK §74, for example, Berkeley talks dismissively of 'I know not what abstracted and indefinite notions of *being*, or *occasion*'. Incidents of this early use of the term 'notion' remain in his revised texts and so it always important to distinguish occurrences of the term 'notion' prior to 1734 and those that occur from that year on.
3 See PHK §46:

> [I]t may to some perhaps seem very incredible, that [in idealism] things should be every moment creating, yet this very notion is commonly taught in the Schools. For the Schoolmen, though they acknowledge the existence of matter, and that the whole mundane fabric is framed out of it, are nevertheless of opinion that it cannot subsist without the divine conservation, which by them is expounded to be a continual creation.

See also PO §6, where God is characterized as the 'maker and preserver or all things', and further suggestions of divine conservation at PHK §147 and §155. For further discussion of this point see Rickless (2016), p. 8.
4 Hegel (1896), vol. 3, particularly pp. 364–5.
5 Fischer (1897–1901); Windelband (1914).
6 Green (1886), Introduction.
7 Russell (1946).
8 Ayer (1980); Urmson (1982).
9 Hegel (1896), vol. 3, p. 364.
10 Muehlmann (1995).
11 Green (1886), pp. 157–8.
12 Ayer (1980), p. 16.
13 See Reid (1863), vol. 1, p. 132.
14 Berkeley, in a letter to the American philosopher Samuel Johnson of 1729, related how he had made 'considerable progress' with a manuscript to Part

II of the *Principles*, but had lost it when travelling in Italy. *Works* II, p. 282. What 'considerable progress' means in this context will always be a matter of speculation.

15 Flage (1987), p. 1. Flage's commitment to the empiricist reading is seen, for example, in the motivation of his rejection of Bracken's innatist interpretation, ibid., pp. 169–80.

16 DHP III 232. Since the publication of his original monograph in 1987, Flage has come to accept that there can be an intuition of the nature of the self on Berkeley's view. 'Intuition', however, does not amount to direct insight into the essential character of the self. Instead, Flage takes the term in Berkeley to mean a theoretical conception which 'philosophers assume as a basis for inquiry'; see Flage (2014), Chapter 6. Knowledge of the nature of the self is therefore still indirect vis-á-vis the thinking substance itself, for it is based on what others have thought and said about the self.

17 See Chapter 3.

18 Pitcher (1977), p. 3.

19 See Berman (1994), pp. 21–2. See also Bettcher (2007), pp. 51–3, and Roberts (2007), p. 90.

20 Roberts (2007), p. 90.

21 PHK §89, emphasis in the original.

22 PHK §142, with my emphasis.

23 PHK §142.

24 See Berman (1994), p. 21. Berman has told me that he had heard Gabriel Moked characterize Berkeley's early period in this way in conversation.

25 *De Motu* is no doubt a transitional work. Doctrinally it seems closest to the writings of the Heroic Period. However, in common with writings in the later phases of his development, Berkeley no longer presents himself as a lone seeker after truth but aligns his doctrine with a tradition stretching back to the pre-Socratics; see Storrie (2012) for discussion.

26 Fraser (1901), vol. 1, p. 338. Berkeley adds statements asserting that relations are notions at PHK §89 and §142.

27 *Siris* §338.

28 *Siris* §335.

29 As G. A. Johnston has it: 'Historically, the relation of *Siris* to Berkeley's early work is one rather of evolution than of revolution. He has travelled far since the days of the *Commonplace Book*, but he has made no volte face. His steps have always been turned in the same direction, and each one of his books marks a stage in his gradual progress.' G. A. Johnston (1923), p. 258.

30 Bracken (1974). A similar reading is offered by Joseph Browne (1975). Another revisionary strand can be found in the work of Stephen M. Daniel and Costica

Bradatan – see Daniel (2001) and (2021), and Bradatan (2006). This credits Berkeley with some form of neo-Platonism from his earliest phase and treats *Siris* and his previous philosophical writings as together expressing one and the same position. My interpretation, in contrast to these, traces Berkeley's intellectual development towards neo-Platonism, rather than attributing to him that position *ab initio*.

31 That is not to say that Berkeley's rejection of the perceptual model was original in the history of philosophy. A *locus classicus* in the ancient world for this view is Plotinus' *Enneads*, V.3.1. Here it is argued that the perceptual model of self-knowledge takes the self to be a compound, allowing one part of the self to perceive another part. This inevitably renders self-knowledge as, at best, partial and incomplete. Plotinus himself holds that the simple self may have complete self-knowledge, but not by any quasi-perceptual act.
32 See Newsome (1974) for an elucidation of the Renaissance concept of *coincidentia oppositorum* which was derived from the thought of Plato.
33 *Siris* §308, emphasis in the original.

2 Berkeley's predecessors on self-knowledge

1 AT VII 181; CSM II 127.
2 See Hatfield (1986), p. 52.
3 Descartes's perceptual model of cognition itself is set forth in Antognazza (2015) and in Ayers and Antognazza (2019), pp. 16–17.
4 It might be noted that Spinoza too follows Descartes in claiming that we have an idea of the mind. Spinoza holds that the mind itself is an idea of the body and self-knowledge therefore involves an idea of an idea. A particular problem that Spinoza faces here concerns his parallelism which asserts that each idea corresponds to a physical state of the body. While the mind is the idea of the body, and therefore corresponds to the whole organism, it is very unclear what the idea of the mind, constituting self-reflective awareness, corresponds to. It is no use saying that it is the whole body again, for that would render it indistinguishable from the mind itself which need not be self-reflective. See particularly *Ethics*, II, Proposition 21.
5 AT VII 28; CSM II 19.
6 AT VII 51; CSM II 35.
7 AT VII 292; CSM II 203.
8 AT VII 367; CSM II 253.
9 PHK §135.

10 AT VII 49; CSM II 34.
11 This problem with an infinite regress is later expressed by Fichte in his introductions to the *Wissenschaftslehre*, see particularly Fichte (1994), p. 112.

> You are conscious of yourself as an object of consciousness only insofar as you are conscious of yourself as the conscious subject; but then this conscious subject becomes, in turn, an object of consciousness, and you must then, once again, become conscious of yourself as the subject who is conscious of this object of consciousness – and so on, ad infinitum. How could you ever arrive at any original consciousness in this way?

12 AT VII 181; CSM II 127.
13 AT XI 343; CSM I 335.
14 Descartes already seemed to unite the idea of willing with the very act of volition in a letter to Mersenne of 28.1.1641: AT III 295; CSMK III 172.
15 For evidence of Berkeley's study of Hobbes' 'Objections' see e.g. Notebooks 795–9.
16 AT VII 183; CSM II 129: AT VII 180; CSM II 127.
17 Hobbes (2012), II, pp. 56–8 (*Leviathan*, I, p. 4).
18 Hobbes (2012), II, p. 22 (*Leviathan*, I, p. 1).
19 Hobbes (2012), II, p. 24 (*Leviathan*, I, p. 1).
20 See Hobbes (2012), III, p. 1030 (*Leviathan*, IV, p. 45).
21 See e.g. Hobbes (2012), II, p. 160 (*Leviathan*, I, p. 11).
22 AT VII 183; CSM II 129.
23 AT VII 185–9; CSM II 130–3.
24 AT VII 189; CSM II 133.
25 Hobbes (1839), vol. I, pp. 392–3.
26 See Malebranche (1997), p. 561 (*Recherche*, Elucidation 3). Malebranche shares the Cartesian general definition of idea, writing in the *Recherche* that 'by the word idea, I mean here nothing other than the immediate object, or the object closest to the mind, when it perceives something, i.e., that which affects and modifies the mind with the perception it has of an object' – Malebranche (1997), p. 217 (*Recherche* III.ii.1). Contained here is a typically Cartesian stress on the perceptual character of ideas. This perceptual theme tends to be overlooked in Nicholas Jolley's Fregean interpretation which takes Malebranchian ideas to be 'abstract logical items to which the mind is related in thinking' (Jolley 1990, p. 87), and which exist in a 'third realm' (see Jolley 2013, pp. 54, 230). Jolley's interpretation passes over the systematic and vivid perceptual language in which the ideas in God are described. Tad Schmaltz, it seems to me, is closer to the truth when he writes that the backbone of Malebranche's doctrine of perception in God

is the 'clear and distinct intellectual perception of the nature of extension' – see Schmaltz (1996), p. 93, and, more generally, pp. 93–124.
27 Malebranche (1997), p. 238.
28 These arguments and others are most explicitly stated in Elucidation 10, see Malebranche (1997), pp. 612–32.
29 Malebranche (1997), p. 238.
30 Ibid., p. 239. The theological questions surrounding our sensation of embodiment are more complex than this, and Malebranche also links the doctrine of '*sentiment intérieur*' with our fallen state.
31 Malebranche (1997), p. 626.
32 Luce (1934), p. 104.
33 Notebooks 230. See also Notebooks 888, where Berkeley rejects Malebranche's doctrine that we know our minds by 'sense or Conscientia', rather than by idea.
34 Malebranche (1997), p. 236.
35 Malebranche (1997), particularly pp. 236–7 (*Recherche* II.ii.7). For an account of Malebranche's direct form of knowledge, as well as his conflicting statements on the subject, see Gueroult (1970), pp. 165–204.
36 PHK §148 and DHP II 214. Berkeley does, however, use Malebranchian language in a looser way, as when he says, for example, that idealism renders God 'intimately present to our minds' (PHK §149).
37 Two examples: 'The grand Mistake' that Berkeley mentions in Notebooks 176a is presented as the Lockean claim that we 'have Ideas of the Operations of our Minds'; and his attack on the (to him) absurd view that we are lacking a sense by which to know substance (PHK §136) is an attack on Locke's empiricist scepticism about substance (as confirmed by Notebooks 601).
38 Locke, *Drafts*, p. 1 ('Draft A', §1).
39 Locke, *Drafts*, p. 7 ('Draft A', §2).
40 E.II.xi.17, p. 163.
41 E.II.i.4, p. 105; and E.II.xi.17, p. 162.
42 E.II.vi.1, p. 127.
43 See E.II.i.8, pp. 107–8; and E.II.xxiii.22, p. 308.
44 E.II.i.25, p. 118.
45 See e.g. E.II.ix.1, p. 143.
46 There is an illuminating discussion of the ambiguities in Locke's view of reflection in D. J. Connor (1952), pp. 104–13. See also Thiel (2011), pp. 121–50 and Hamou (2018), p. 128.
47 E II.i.19, p. 115. See also E.II.xxvii.9, p. 335, where Locke talks of our 'perceiving' that we are perceiving.
48 See E.II.i.8, pp. 107–8.

49 Shelley Weinberg (2016), pp. 40–3, has argued that Locke distinguishes between mere consciousness of our mental activities and the acquisition of ideas of those activities by reflection. We can be conscious, fleetingly and confusedly, of a mental operation, on this interpretation, without fixing our attention on it and forming an idea of reflection. Only when we begin to reflect on our operations with attention, do we gain ideas of them. As reflection is a power that is acquired in the course of growing up, very young children do not even have evanescent ideas of reflection according to Weinberg. However, Locke does make statements that are hard to square with Weinberg's interpretation. For example, he characterizes ideas as 'whatsoever the Mind perceives in it self [i.e. in the mind]' (E.II.viii.8, p. 134, see also E. 'Epistle to the Reader', p. 14). This characterization seems to leave no room for any alleged fleeting conscious perceptions of one's mental operations that somehow do not qualify as ideas.
50 E.II.i.4, p. 105.
51 E.II.i.4, pp. 105–6.
52 E.II.vii.1–2, pp. 128–9; E.II.xx.1, p. 229.
53 E.II.vii.1, p. 128; E.II.xxi.73, p. 287; E.II.xxviii.14, p. 358.
54 E.II.xxi.4, p. 235: 'If we will consider it attentively, Bodies, by our Senses, do not afford us so clear and distinct an *Idea* of *active Power*, as we have from reflection on the Operations of our Minds.'
55 E.II.xxiii.29, p. 312.
56 E.II.xxiii.32, p. 313.
57 E.II.xxiii.15, pp. 305–6, emphasis in the original.
58 The suggestion of a Spinozist subtext was first insinuated by Edward Stillingfleet, but was systematically set out by William Carroll. Carroll, a High Church Irishman, argued that Locke's sceptical stance towards the real essence of both material and spiritual substance tacitly signalled acceptance of the identification of God with the universe – see Carroll (1705), pp. 4–5. Carroll then went on to offer evidence that Locke did indeed affirm Spinoza's identification of God and universe, pointing to the distinction between nominal and real essences (E.III.iii.13), the 'thinking matter' passage (E.IV.iii.6) and, most importantly, to the discussion of the possibility that God is material in the chapter 'Of Our Knowledge of the Existence of a God' (E.IV.x.) – see Carroll (1705), pp. 10–11, 42, and Carroll (1706), *passim*. Carroll's reading has recently been sympathetically treated in Kim (2019).
59 E.IV.iii.6, p. 540. Leibniz treated Locke as a crypto-materialist – see Leibniz and Clarke (1956), p. 11.
60 E.IV.iii.6, pp. 540–1.
61 See Wilson (1979) and Ayers (1991), vol. 2, pp. 169–83.

62 Locke's seeming concession that 'the more probable Opinion is, that this consciousness is annexed to, and the Affection of one individual immaterial Substance' (E.II.xxvii.25, p. 345) should not be taken as an abandonment of this agnosticism. This is partly because of the context, in which he goes straight on to dismiss the whole question of the immaterial soul as one of 'divers Hypotheses' (where 'hypothesis' means something like unfounded supposition), but also because, on Locke's own view, the term 'probability' incorporates 'the testimony of others' and 'the number' of witnesses (see E.IV.xv.5), and he is therefore best understood as noting the 'received opinion' when he was writing. As Kim (2019) points out, 'what Locke assents to is simply the *historical fact* that the immateriality of the soul is the more popular opinion of his time' (p. 46).

63 E.IV.x.10, p. 624. It should be emphasized that Locke's assertion that God is immaterial and cannot therefore be constituted by 'incogitative matter' does little or nothing to make more probable the human mind's immateriality. This is because, as Philippe Hamou has pointed out, God's thinking is a necessary part of his nature, while man's thinking – interrupted and intermittent as it is – is only contingently related to the nature of the human mind. As Hamou concludes, 'the argument for God's immateriality does not fit, even analogically, when applied to man.' See Hamou (2006), p. 19.

64 E.IV.iii.6, p. 542.

65 Notebooks 695. See also Notebooks 718.

3 A notion of an active self

1 PHK §142.

2 Locke, E.I.i.5, pp. 45–6. See also E.IV.iii.6, p. 542, where Locke writes that 'all the great Ends of Morality and Religion, are well enough secured, without philosophical Proofs of the Soul's Immateriality'.

3 The close union of the mind with the body, which results from our lack of a clear idea of our spiritual self, is, however, a matter of theological complexity for Malebranche. On the one hand, the union has a benign role in inciting us to protect and sustain our bodily selves. But, in our fallen state, the close union also tends to blind us to our union with God and can result in our being enslaved to sensuality. See Malebranche (1997), pp. 19–24 (*Recherche*, I.5)

4 PHK §135.

5 PHK Intro §4. Margaret Atherton (2020), p. 106, captures the import of Berkeley's thinking here when she says that 'in the case of spirits, the problem is

not that we think we know more than we actually do, but that the knowledge we do have is better than we think it is'.
6 PHK §137.
7 There is a droll reference to the title of Sergeant's book at Notebooks 840.
8 Sergeant (1697), p. 23, emphasis in the original.
9 Notebooks 657a. This comment was retrospectively added to the manuscript as a comment on 657 and it may have been made after he read Sergeant (who is mentioned in Notebooks 840).
10 PHK §141.
11 See Luce (1934), p. 72; Leroy (1959), pp. 101–3; Winkler (1989), pp. 53–75; Roberts (2007), pp. 32–4. Simple ideas are portrayed as abstract ideas at PHK Intro §7 and are therefore rejected in the ensuing attack on abstraction. For the opposing view, which treats Berkeley as clinging onto simple ideas until the Middle Period, see Berman (2015), pp. 18–20. At Siris §347, Berkeley writes that 'upon mature reflection the person or mind of all created beings seemeth alone indivisible, and to partake most of unity'. This statement, Berman has suggested to me, looks to indicate that it was only in the later phase of his career – characterized by 'mature reflection' – that he dropped simplicity in things other than mind. I would argue that the 'mature reflection' came earlier in his philosophical development.
12 NTV §54.
13 Atoms at least have parts in the sense that we can in principle distinguish between areas of the surface (say, the left-hand side and the right-hand side).
14 Malebranche, the other sceptic, remarks early on in the *Recherche* that the soul is indivisible (Malebranche 1997, p. 2), but makes no mention of this indivisibility when he comes to talk in detail of our knowledge of the soul by a '*sentiment intérieur*' (ibid., pp. 237–9, 633–8).
15 See his letter to Percival of 27.12.1709 in Berkeley (2013), pp. 31–4, where he extols Socrates, on the basis of the *Phaedo*, as 'the most admirable man that the heathen world produced'. Although Berkeley was in his mid-twenties at the time of the letter, he tells Percival 'it is now years since I read this dialogue'. The *Phaedo* – along with the *Theaetetus* and the *Timaeus* – is central to Berkeley's interpretation of Plato in *Siris* – see, for example, *Siris* §260.
16 See A. A. Luce's discussion of this issue at Luce (1953), p. 20.
17 PHK §25.
18 PHK §25.
19 PHK §25, with my emphasis.
20 PHK §31.
21 PHK §32.
22 PHK §28; DM §25, §30.

23 PHK §27, emphasis in the original.
24 PHK Intro §2.
25 Pitcher (1977), p. 222; see more generally pp. 211–23. Pitcher allows that knowledge of the *existence* of my spirit may be immediate, but its nature is known only relatively.
26 See e.g. PHK §2.
27 See Flage (2004), pp. 32–4.
28 Flage (1987), p. 152. Keota Fields (2011), pp. 119–20, adopts Flage's interpretation.
29 DHP III 231.
30 DHP III 231. See also DM §§21, 30.
31 For valuable critiques of Pitcher's original claim see Atherton (1983), p. 339 (including note 6), and Sukjae Lee (2012), pp. 557–9. Flage has more recently modified his view. In Flage (2014), chapter 6, he allows that an intuition of the self is possible, where 'intuition' refers to a presupposed conception, common to philosophers. Intuition in this sense does not, however, amount to direct experiential insight into the nature of the self.
32 PHK §86.
33 DHP I 204.
34 NTV §§9–10.
35 *Siris* §308.
36 See PHK §2; DM §30; *Siris* §308.
37 Winkler (2011), p. 230. See also Tipton (1974), pp. 266–7, who talks about mental action, on Berkeley's view, as something 'we are aware of through doing it'; and Pearce (2017), who writes that 'actions are known in the doing of them'.
38 DHP III 233.
39 This misapprehension is also addressed by Ian Tipton who dismissed it as 'a dualism between notions on the one hand and spirit and acts on the other', see Tipton (1974), p. 270. A. D. Woozley wrote, in a similar vein, that 'we do not now have *three* kinds of thing in the world, minds, ideas *and* notions', see Woozley (1976), p. 430, emphasis in the original.
40 We should not forget that there do remain some ideas of the 'inner' sphere for Berkeley, in addition to notions. We have feelings of, say, uneasiness or satisfaction which are presumably passive ideas of inner states which accompany our mental activities. Arguably, it is these residual ideas of reflection that Berkeley is referring to at PHK §1, where he seems to endorse ideas of reflection, before he sets out the knowledge of spiritual substance and its activities at PHK §2. See Pearce (2017), chapter 7.
41 Fichte (1994), p. 46.
42 Malebranche (1997), pp. 236–7.

43 Notebooks 176 (with punctuation added to indicate a sentence break). Cf. also Notebooks 490.
44 Notebooks 176a.
45 DM §3. Whether Berkeley himself is always able to escape metaphor is, however, another question. See Tomeček (2015), pp. 29–30, for the claim that the words 'external' and 'internal', which literally refer to the spatial domain, are employed in Berkeley's immaterialism in a systematically metaphorical way.
46 PHK §144.
47 AT VII 181; CSM II 127.
48 PHK §89.
49 T 251–63 (Book I, part iv, section 6).
50 T 252.
51 Ibid.
52 See T 254. Also see Wright (2009), p. 163.
53 See Strawson (2011), p. 75, for the interpretation of 'perception' as 'episode of perceiving'.
54 T 252.
55 Notebooks 580, 577.
56 I join with most commentators who regard these remarks in the Notebooks as anticipating the position made famous by David Hume in his *Treatise*. Stephen Daniel, however, has developed an alternative, non-Humean, reading in Daniel (2010, 2013) and most recently in Daniel (2021), pp. 94–6. He treats entries 577–81 as maintaining a theory of spiritual substance 'in a Neoplatonic sense' (p. 95) and, as such, perfectly compatible with Berkeley's later, published doctrine. Crucial to Daniel's interpretation is his reading of the phrase 'congeries of Perceptions' in entry 580 as employing the term 'perception' in the sense of *act of* perceiving, not idea perceived. However, this reading has two vulnerabilities. Firstly, in the light of neighbouring entries, it seems highly probable that Berkeley does indeed mean 'perception' in the sense of idea perceived. At 577, for example, he frames the 'congeries of Perceptions' claim in terms of ideas, stating that 'the very existence of Ideas constitutes the soul'; and at 587 the term 'idea' is used, indifferently, as an alternative for 'perception'. Secondly, it becomes apparent in entry 579 that Berkeley, in this episode of his development, takes the mind to be *perceivable* – as indeed it must be if it is constituted by ideas. Entry 579 presents the reader with the alternative of treating the mind as something perceived or as something not perceived, immediately going on to disqualify the second option altogether as 'a contradiction', leaving the mind as necessarily something perceived. The perceptibility of the mind is not only in conflict with the neo-Platonist understanding of spiritual substance that Daniel attributes to Berkeley in the Notebooks, it is also a doctrine that Berkeley goes on to categorically reject

in his later published work, as stated, for example, at DHP 231. Daniel's non-Humean reading of 577–81 overlooks this crucial shift on the perceptibility of mind in Berkeley's early development. The shift is starkly visible in a comparison of Notebooks 581 and PHK §2: where once Berkeley dismissed as 'empty words' the characterization of the mind as 'that thing which perceives', he later asserts that mind is, indeed, 'a thing ... whereby [ideas] are perceived'.

57 Notebooks 579 (with question mark added).
58 Notebooks 587.
59 Notebooks 645.
60 Notebooks 657.
61 Notebooks 708.
62 Notebooks 806, 847.
63 This comment is numbered 176a and, although in published versions of the Notebooks it comes near the beginning, it is of course a later addition to the text, going further than the original entry 176, which had only rejected any general parallel between our understanding of sense and the spiritual. Now Berkeley wishes to stress that we must even abandon all talk of ideas when treating of mental operations.
64 Notebooks 806. I suspect that the retrospective 176a was made around the same time as this entry.
65 See e.g. PHK §89.
66 PHK §22, emphasis in the original.
67 Samuel Alexander distinguished between 'contemplation' and 'enjoyment', using these two terms in a way that is only distantly related to their meanings in ordinary language. Contemplation characterizes our consciousness of the objects of our mental operations – what they are about. 'Enjoyment', on the other hand, refers to the experience of our operations on the object contemplated. Alexander writes: 'The mind enjoys itself and contemplates its objects. The act of mind is an enjoyment; the object is contemplated.' Alexander (1927), p. 12. See Lloyd (1985), p. 202, for a parallel suggestion drawing on the distinction in German between *Wahrnehmen* (contemplation) and *Erleben* (enjoyment or lived experience).
68 For a useful discussion of these issues see Dicker (2011), pp. 210–23. Dicker is sympathetic to the non-perceptual reading of notions in Berkeley, and he thinks the position makes philosophical sense of self-knowledge. He comments: 'As I think through an argument, I am not aware of a thinker distinct from the thinking, but just of the thinking, and arguably that awareness is a case of direct acquaintance with myself' (ibid., p. 223).
69 PHK §27. The reference to 'understanding' here, in this sentence added in 1734, seems to be in tension with the claim earlier in the section that the understanding is limited to 'perceiving ideas'.

70 A purist version of this theory is to be found in Geach (1960), p. 12, where it is claimed that 'if [one] knows how to use the first-person pronoun, [one] has a concept of self'. For discussion and rejection of such an interpretation of Berkeley see Jaffro (2004).

71 Pearce (2017), chapter 7; Woozley (1976), p. 434. While Woozley recognizes that the term 'mind' and the different terms for mental operations do denote, he does also chide Berkeley with not being 'tidy enough in his presentation', and of sometimes talking as if mind were 'a non-denoting theoretical term' (pp. 433–4).

72 E. III.ii.1, p. 405.

73 E. III.vii.1, p. 471.

74 One should exclude 662 and 664 from this sequence, for they discuss the theory of vision. One should also be aware of the relevance of the entries 657–60 which precede. These argue against there being any idea of the will, a theme then taken up in reference to Locke's semantics in the series of entries under discussion.

75 Notebooks 717.

4 Notions and innatism

1 PHK §89, §142 (second edition).

2 *Siris* §308. Sameness had already been discussed in the Third Dialogue, where Berkeley pointed to the lack of a clear univocal meaning. The addition of relations, of which sameness is clearly one, to the list of notions in the Middle Period, and the explicit reference to 'parity' in *Siris*, therefore indicates a crucial expansion of the doctrine of notions. I shall discuss this in Chapter 8.

3 Augustine (1997), p. 251 (*Confessions*, Book 10, chapter xvi, p. 22). In this passage, Augustine is speaking of the emotions of desire, joy, fear and sadness. He also talks of *notiones* in connection with ideas such as happiness and wisdom, where again there is no corporeal image.

4 O'Daly (1987), p. 184.

5 James (1997), p. 114. Peter Geach suggested that Berkeley's use of the term 'notion' may be connected with Augustine's *notiones* – see Geach (1971), p. 108.

6 For treatments of Descartes's special use of the term '*notio*', see Hart (1970); Beck (1965), pp. 88–92; Marion (1991), pp. 96–101.

7 See *Principles* I, 10: AT VIIIA 8; CSM I 196.

8 The title of the First Book of Locke's *Essay* often goes unnoticed because it only appears on the page of contents, and not in the text proper. See *Essay*, p. 15.

9 These phrases occur, for example, at E.I.ii.1, p. 48; E.I.ii.5, pp. 49–5; E.I.iii.16, p. 77, as well as elsewhere in the First Book of the *Essay*. The term 'notion' is also,

of course, to be found in a looser sense, in both Locke and Berkeley, referring to an opinion or intellectual idea.
10 See DHP I 193–4; DM §53.
11 See ALC I, 14–15, pp. 55–60; OWG 130–1; *Siris* §309.
12 Urmson (1982), p. 110.
13 Notebooks 717.
14 Notebooks 649.
15 Although Stephen Daniel has argued for an innatist reading of Berkeley from the Notebooks onwards in Daniel (2010), see particularly pp. 8–10.
16 See Ayers (2005), p. 48, for this kind of deflationary reading. He comments: 'If a soul's *esse* is *percipere*, then at least one idea must be perceived in its first moment of existence.'
17 AT VII 51; CSM II 35.
18 Locke discusses a subtler, implicit, form of innatism at, for example, E.I.ii.22, pp. 59–60.
19 E I.ii.1, p. 48. See also E. II.i.1, p. 104, where Locke again talks of men having 'Characters stamped upon their Minds'. Throughout his polemic in the First Book of the *Essay* he uses physical metaphors of characters being 'impressed', 'imprinted', 'engraven' or 'inscribed' on the mind. A typical formulation is at E. I.iii.15, p. 77, where he characterizes Herbert of Cherbury's view as claiming that 'common Notions [are] imprinted on the Minds of Men by the Hand of God.' Berkeley discusses this metaphorical language of stamping and engraving in his *Passive Obedience*, where he reinterprets it – and endorses it – as meaning 'suggested and inculcated by Conscience' (PO §12).
20 Locke, Corres. 4. L 1544, p. 535.
21 AT VIIIB 358; CSM I 303: 'I have never written or taken the view that the mind requires innate ideas which are something distinct from its own faculty of thinking.' See also AT VII 189; CSM II 133; AT VII 372–4; CSM II 256–7.
22 See AT VIIIB 358–9; CSM I 304, where Descartes goes as far as to treat ideas of sensations, or what we call 'secondary qualities', as generated internally, and thus 'innate'.
23 See Leibniz (1996), pp. 110–11; Leibniz (1998), p. 261 (*Principles of Nature and Grace* §5), p. 272 (*Monadology* §30).
24 Leibniz (1996), p. 111.
25 Ibid.
26 Nicholas Jolley treats the reflection account as unqualified to be a true innatist theory because 'it is clear that this is not an innate disposition in the sense of one we have possessed since birth' (1990, pp. 182–3). However, while it is highly unlikely that an infant would undertake the reflection involved, clearly the potential for reflection is present from the beginning in rational beings, and this

is surely enough to make it an innatist theory. As Descartes points out, congenital gout is not found in the neonate but it is still said to be innate in certain families because of its potential to develop, at a later age, in the individuals affected (AT VIIIB 361; CSM I 305). The crucial point is that the very nature of the mind, from its beginning, is the source of the potential for reflective knowledge of these innate concepts.

27 AT VII 67; CSM II 46.
28 Malebranche (1997), p. 227. Malebranche himself was not drawn to the self-reflection theory of innatism, but rather to his doctrine of seeing all things in God. The self-reflection theory would not find any appeal in Malebranche because he was concerned above all with intelligible extension which could hardly be thought to arise in this way. In addition, Malebranche would shun such a theory because of his Augustinian conviction that the mind is not a light unto itself, and thus all cognitive enlightenment must issue straight from God Himself (see ibid., pp. 622–4).
29 Flage is clearly thinking of the crude version of innatism when he describes it as 'contrary to Berkeley's arguments from parsimony'. See Flage (1987), p. 180.
30 A point stressed by Ayers (2005), p. 40.
31 See, particularly, his discussion of space in the Fifth Letter to Clarke, p. 47, Leibniz (1956), pp. 69–72, and the comment, in the *New Essays*, that 'the idea of extension is posterior to those of whole and part', Leibniz (1996), p. 103.
32 DM §53.
33 Notebooks 775.
34 *Siris* §308.
35 DM §§71–2 (PW, 275–6).
36 PHK §16, §49. See also *Siris* §337.
37 *Siris* §309.
38 *Siris* §309. It should be noted that the expression 'to explode' here was a popular one in the theatre at this time referring to cases where the audience drives an actor from the stage by hoots and jeers.
39 Notebooks 650–2, quoting 652.
40 See also Notebooks 704.
41 *Monadology* §30; Leibniz (1998), p. 272.
42 Leibniz (1996), pp. 51, 105, 111.
43 ALC I, 14–15, pp. 55–60; OWG 130–1.
44 PHK §23.
45 In *De motu*, for example, Berkeley more than once talks of our experience of causal power. See, for example, DM §30, where he writes, 'A thinking, active thing is given which we experience as the principle of motion in ourselves.'
46 E.II.i.2, p. 104.

47 Grayling (2005), p. 173.
48 Leibniz treats our knowledge of substance to be gained 'from the intimate *experience* of our own self' (*ex intima nostri ipsius experientia*), see Leibniz (1948), II, p. 558 (with my emphasis).
49 Gassendi draws on *le sens intime* in resisting Descartes's pure intellect; see, for example, Gassendi (1962), p. 166.
50 AT VII 28; CSM II 19.
51 Ryle (1963), p. 187.
52 Leibniz (1996), p. 109.
53 Leibniz (1962), p. 14 ('*Échantillon des Réflexions sur l'Essay*', Livre II).
54 Leibniz (1948), II, p. 558. This unpublished manuscript is dated 'after November 1704', and thus after his reading of Locke in Pierre Coste's French translation. The term *notitia* is, like *notio*, derived from *noscere*.
55 As in Kant's famous dictum at CPR, B 131, 'It must be possible for the "I think" to accompany all my representations [*Vorstellungen*].'
56 Carl Stumpf (1939), p. 342.
57 DM §21. See also PHK §89 where Berkeley talks of 'inward feeling'.
58 PHK §7.
59 See also DHP III 231.
60 See Notebooks 779, where he employs this principle to critique abstract ideas, still recognizing knowledge of the active will in nearby entries (see e.g. 756 and 777). His point is that so far as objects in the intellect are concerned – that is, ideas – all are derived from sense. At Notebooks 819, he notes that Descartes means by idea any object in the mind (*objectivum in Intellectu*).
61 See Winkler (1989), pp. 232–3.
62 *Siris* §335.
63 Fichte (1994), p. 47.
64 Mill (1969), p. 120.

5 Sense perception: A passive or an active power?

1 PHK §29.
2 PHK §28.
3 AT VII 79; CSM II 55.
4 Ibid.
5 PHK §27. See also PHK §138 where Berkeley sees sense perception as an active power.
6 DHP I 194–7.

7. DHP I 194.
8. Ibid.
9. DHP I 195.
10. Gilbert Ryle (1963), p. 145.
11. Charles McCracken (1986), p. 152. Attempts have been made to meet the challenge that McCracken poses both before and after his statement of it. Anita D. Fritz resisted the split by arguing that the self is both passive and active in perception: passive because it cannot determine the content of the perceptions, but active because it is 'conscious or aware of perceived content', see Fritz (1954), p. 560. Margaret Atherton (2010) also argues that Berkeley ultimately assumes an activity of 'present attentiveness' which accompanies all perception, despite the passivity of its content. In both these interpretations, the split can never open up because all passive mental states are at once active too. The interpretation I offer in this chapter will also assert that passivity and activity are inextricably bound up with one another, but the kind of activity in question will be different to the active attention that Fritz and Atherton both have in mind.
12. Berkeley's subjective theory of time is one of the most remarkable parts of his philosophy. By denying that periods of non-consciousness are part of the subjective temporal continuum, Berkeley can defend his claim that the mind is always and essentially active. The peculiar difficulties that this theory creates lie beyond the scope of this monograph. Perhaps the most convincing attempt to make sense of Berkeley's theory of time is offered in Bettcher (2007), chapter 6, who argues that ideas, but not spirits, are part of the temporal course of nature. A spirit witnesses this course 'without being part of it', and a spirit as 'the required centre of temporal elapse' undergoes no change (p. 99).
13. DHP I 196.
14. Notebooks 155.
15. Notebooks 821. This may be a rare approving nod to Locke who tells us that perception, along with volition, are the 'two great and principal Actions of the Mind' (E. II.vi.2, p. 128).
16. Notebooks 841. See also Notebooks 833 and 854.
17. Smelling, of course, involves the muscular exertion of breathing in.
18. See Locke, E. II.xxi.5, p. 236 and E II.xxi.28, p. 248, where he stresses forbearance in his definition of will. Anthony Collins defines will as the 'power of the man … to order the beginning or forbearance, the continuance or ending of any action', in Collins (1717), p. 37. Berkeley would have certainly known Locke's definition of will and his treatment of forbearance. The book by Collins was, however, published four years later than the *Three Dialogues*, and I wish only to contrast the definitions of will in each.
19. DHP 1 195.

20 AT VI 109; CSM I 164. Margaret Atherton points to the relevance of this passage in Descartes when highlighting the active aspect of perception in Berkeley – see Atherton (2010), p. 125.
21 E.II.xix.1, p. 227.
22 E.II.xix.3, p. 228.
23 Notebooks 791.
24 NTV §§109–10.
25 PHK §12.
26 Gravity is also added to the list of primary qualities at DHP I, 187–8.
27 A useful discussion of Berkeley's views on number which pays particular attention to *Siris* is to be found in Roberts (2007), pp. 28–32. Roberts argues that 'Berkeley works in sympathy with that aspect of the Platonic tradition that identifies *ens* with *unum*' (p. 29), and *unum* arises from an act of mind.
28 *Siris* §288.
29 PHK §12.
30 *Siris* §355.
31 *Siris* §356.
32 Kant, CPR, B131–6.
33 Kant, CPR, B406–33.
34 DHP I 201.
35 DHP I 202.
36 DHP III 249.
37 See Roberts (2007), pp. 31–2, for an enlightening discussion of this passage.
38 Margaret Atherton (2020), p. 180, argues that Berkeley's claim here in the *Three Dialogues* that he is 'not for changing things into ideas, but rather ideas into things' (DHP III 244) is to be understood along these lines. It is the claim that the human mind, by attaching names to groups of co-existing and succeeding ideas, actively makes them into more than just ideas, considering them now as 'one thing'. 'Humans', she writes, 'may be said to be in the business of turning ideas into things.'
39 PHK §2.
40 Brykman (1985), p. 128.
41 See *Siris* §355.

6 Berkeley's conceptual dynamism

1 Berkeley treated Cartesians, like scholastics and empiricists, as targets of his attack on abstract ideas (see Notebooks 811).

2 Descartes has this kind of abstraction in mind when he talks of simpler things being more universal at CSM II 14 and AT VII 20.
3 For Berkeley's characterization of simple ideas as abstractions see PHK intro §7. It is interesting to compare this section of Berkeley's published introduction with its precursor in the Draft Introduction, which does not target simple ideas and where, indeed, no mention is made of simplicity at all (see Draft Introduction, p. 123). It seems likely that Berkeley came to consciously reject the Lockean doctrine of simple ideas sometime between the writing of these two differently worded accounts of the 'singling out' of abstract ideas. He thus came to reject simple ideas that had been endorsed in the Notebooks (see e.g. entry 378). For a thorough examination of Berkeley's rejection of simple ideas, and on the development of his thought in this regard, see Winkler (1989), pp. 53–75.
4 PHK §§8–9.
5 PHK Intro 13.
6 For this theme see PHK §§97–8; PHK §100.
7 PHK §5.
8 PHK Intro 17.
9 E.II.xi.9, p. 159.
10 See E.II.i.22, p. 117; E.II.xi.8–10, pp. 158–60.
11 See E.II.xii.1, p. 163.
12 E.II.viii.8, p. 134.
13 PHK I §18.
14 PHK Intro 12.
15 Jerry Fodor has distinguished between two approaches to the question of concept possession – representationalism and pragmatism (see e.g. Fodor [2003], pp. 14–17). Representationalism, which Fodor ascribes to Descartes, Hume and to himself, holds that a concept is an object standing before the mind presenting a certain content, and that the relations perceived between such objects amount to propositions. Pragmatism, on the other hand, which Fodor ascribes to Wittgenstein, Ryle, Sellars, Dummett and (with certain reservations) Heidegger, treats a concept as a skill or technique. The pragmatist takes the content of a concept to arise inter alia from our intelligent activity. Berkeley, who is not discussed by Fodor, would, I think, belong among the pragmatists.
16 T 17, emphasis in the original.
17 T 20.
18 See Garrett (1997), pp. 102–4.
19 T 21.
20 PHK Intro §16.
21 PHK Intro §16.

22 See Notebooks 104, 110 and 318 for this kind of active use of to 'consider', implying much more than merely perceiving ideas.
23 T 21.
24 Ibid.
25 T 24.
26 Hobbes (2012), p. 52 (*Leviathan*, I, 4).
27 Ibid., p. 54 (*Leviathan*, I, 4).
28 PHK Intro §13.
29 PHK Intro §12.
30 Warnock (1982), pp. 71–2.
31 PHK Intro §12.
32 PHK Intro §15.
33 PHK Intro §16.
34 That 'to consider' means something more than 'to carefully perceive' for Berkeley is clear from Notebooks 104, 110 and 318.
35 Ryle (1963), p. 27.
36 PHK §89.
37 PHK §142.
38 PHK Intro §15, with my emphasis.
39 Fraser (1901), I, p. 338. What Fraser sees, Bertrand Russell misses. Russell overlooks Berkeley's treatment of relations when he talks of Kant as the first to claim that 'relations are the work of the mind' (Russell 1967, p. 51).
40 Notebooks 775.
41 DHP I 193–4: 'Since I cannot frame abstract ideas at all, it is plain, I cannot frame them by the help *of pure intellect*, whatsoever faculty you understand by those words.'
42 *Siris* §308.

7 A notion of goodness

1 *Siris* §308.
2 *Theaetetus* 185^d–186^a.
3 *Theaetetus* 185^e.
4 *Siris* §331, see also §350 and PHK §156. Sadducism had become synonymous among Cambridge Platonists with the rejection of spirit and with a range of sins, both intellectual and moral, which were deemed to go with this rejection, including the denial of free will.
5 Notebooks 508.

6 Notebooks 669.
7 Notebooks 684.
8 Notebooks 683, 691.
9 DHP I 194.
10 See also DHP I 174, where it is agreed, by both parties to the dialogue, that it would be absurd to say that virtue is a 'sensible thing' or perceived by sense.
11 PO §13.
12 I do not think that Berkeley rejects moral sense theory primarily for being 'subjective', as has been argued by Airaksinen (2016), p. 219, so much as for being contemplative or 'indolent', and thus as inimical to active engagement in the world.
13 Notebooks 176a.
14 See Glauser (2002).
15 Shaftesbury (2000), pp. 326–7.
16 ALC VII, x, *Works*, III, 303. Berkeley provides an extended and systematic critique of moral sense theory in Dialogue III of *Alciphron*.
17 *Siris* §335.
18 See, for example, Rickless (2016), pp. 10–14, where Berkeley is treated as offering a sophisticated position that combines act-utilitarianism (in relation to the standard of appraising the goodness of an action) with rule-utilitarianism (in relation to the decision procedure for determining which action to pursue at a given moment). Incidentally, I am assuming that 'utilitarianism' is, by definition, a form of hedonistic ethics and that it goes beyond bare consequentialism by filling in a conception of the good with pleasure, happiness or *eudaimonia*. Thus defined, I hold, Berkeley is not a utilitarian.
19 Rickless (2016); Darwall (2005).
20 Berman (1986), p. 313.
21 Mill (1919), p. 621.
22 PO §6. The Notebooks do seem to defend a form of hedonism (see particularly, entries 542, 769 and 773). Perhaps the development of an individual's conception of the moral good away from hedonism described here represents Berkeley's own intellectual path.
23 PO §6. This is a point stressed by Berman (1986), p. 313. As Berman points out, the theological character of well-being means that any suffering on earth can be cancelled by rewards in the afterlife.
24 PO §5. This may also have some autobiographical significance, as in the Notebooks the more youthful Berkeley had written of sensual pleasure that it constitutes the '*Summum Bonum*' (Notebooks 769). It should be noted here that 'sensual pleasure' should not be taken to mean 'bodily pleasure' which can be contemptible for bringing pain in its wake (see Notebooks 773), but rather the

aesthetic pleasures of, say, visual art and music (see Notebooks 774) which 'surfeit not' and do not 'bring evils after them'.

25 Daniel Flage (2014), chapter 7, has also rejected the utilitarian reading, but for rather different reasons. He argues that Berkeley is a theological natural law theorist. While the natural laws laid down by God do maximize the well-being of mankind, they do this 'distributively' not merely 'collectively'. For this reason, Flage argues, a caste system, in which the suffering of those in a lower caste might maximize overall happiness by enabling the abundant pleasures of those in a higher caste, could never be treated as legitimate in Berkeley's conception, though it must be recommended by the thoroughgoing utilitarian.

26 PO §12. See Häyry (2012), pp. 12–13, for an interpretation which makes conscience the crucial guide to understanding right action in Berkeley's conception of ethics and which treats conscience as 'spiritual reason'.

27 *Works* VII, 227.
28 *Works* VII, 227; PO §5.
29 *Siris* §342.
30 *Siris* §259. The emotion of love is known by notion because it is an operation, or active power, rather than a passion in any literal sense (PHK §27).
31 *Siris* §259.
32 *Siris* §260.
33 *Siris* §342.
34 *Siris* §347.
35 PHK §12.
36 NTV §109.
37 *Siris* §356.

8 Number and the notion of God

1 PHK §§119–22.
2 See Jesseph (1993). Jesseph is most concerned to develop a formalist interpretation of Berkeley's view of arithmetic, treating him as the first in a line which goes on to include Eduard Heine and David Hilbert. Jesseph does, however, also make useful comments on the first question of how we arrive at unity and the number one (see particularly pp. 95–106).
3 E. II.vii.7, p. 131.
4 Notebooks 746.
5 Notebooks 104.
6 Notebooks 110.

7 NTV §109.
8 PHK §12.
9 *Siris* §288.
10 Frege (1986), p. 33.
11 *Siris* §356.
12 DHP III 231–2.
13 DHP III 241.
14 'Impassive' in the sense of lacking passivity. See DHP II 213, where God is characterized as 'an impassive, indivisible, purely active being'.
15 Locke explains how we gain our conception of God at E.II.xxiii.33–6, pp. 314–16.
16 Grayling (1986), p. 187.
17 See the editor's footnote at DHP III 232, which reads 'Berkeley is here following Locke (*Essay* xxiii 33–5), who rejects Descartes' doctrine of the innateness of the idea of God and the consequent priority of the idea of perfection over that of imperfection.'
18 PHK §101.
19 See, for example, Notebooks 154, where Berkeley still seems to be happy to talk of ideas of the soul.
20 E. II.xxiii.34, p. 315.
21 E. II.xxiii.35, p. 315.
22 Notebooks 104.
23 See *Siris* §§345–6, where this view is rendered in a neo-Platonist framework, with the unity of the human mind being owed to the participation of the divine mind.
24 See Examination §31 and §50, p.438 and pp. 449–50.
25 That this doctrine is an important consideration in Berkeley's discussion is revealed by an article he published in the *Guardian* in 1713 (article XII), the same year as the *Three Dialogues*: 'I regard my own soul as the image of her Creator, and receive great consolation from beholding those perfections which testify her divine original, and lead me into some knowledge of her everlasting archetype' (*Works* VII, 222).
26 While Browne allowed a certain 'analogical' understanding of God's attributes by reference to human powers, King was more sceptical, denying that our powers have even a modicum of likeness to the divine. See Storrie (2022).
27 AT VII 51; CSM II 35.
28 AT VII 373; CSM II 257.
29 AT VII 51; CSM II 35.
30 Notebooks 176.
31 Malebranche was able to say of God that 'I directly perceive his being', but Berkeley would be opposed to this view as indicated in the First Dialogue where he goes out of his way to state that virtue, reason and God cannot be perceived.

This, of course, is tied up with Berkeley's narrow understanding of perception as having only the images of sense as its objects.
32 DHP III 194 (italics in the original).
33 Roberts (2007), p. 37. See, more generally, the discussion on pages 35–7, where Roberts equates Berkeley's pure intellect with Descartes's. But, against the Cartesian reading, one should remember that Berkeley would object to the very possibility of our *perceiving* ideas of ourselves, or of God, no matter how intellectual and non-sensory those ideas were intended to be. It would be hard to improve on Luce's cautious verdict: '[Berkeley] never admits "pure intellect" as a faculty of abstraction, but, I think, he never denied "pure intellect" as a faculty of the supersensible.' Luce (1934), p. 116.
34 DM §53.

Bibliography

Works by Berkeley

1989. *Philosophical Commentaries*, edited by George H. Thomas. New York: Garland.
1901. *The Works of George Berkeley D. D.; Formerly Bishop of Cloyne*, vols I–IV, edited by A. C. Fraser. Oxford: Clarendon (reprinted by Bristol: Thoemmes, 1994).
1948-51. *The Works of George Berkeley*, edited by A. A. Luce and T. E. Jessop. London: Thomas Nelson.
2008. *George Berkeley: Philosophical Writings*, edited by Desmond M. Clarke. Cambridge: Cambridge University Press.
2013. *The Correspondence of George Berkeley*, edited by Marc Hight. Cambridge: Cambridge University Press.

Works by Others

Airaksinen, Timo. 2016. 'Idealistic Ethics and Berkeley's Good God', in Joshua Farris and Mark Hamilton (eds), *Idealism and Christian Theory*, vol. 1, 217–35. New York: Bloomsbury.
Alexander, Samuel. 1927. *Space, Time and Deity: The Gifford Lectures at Glasgow, 1916-18*. In two volumes. London: Macmillan.
Alquié, Ferdinand. 1974. *Le Cartésianisme de Malebranche*. Paris: J. Vrin.
Alweiss, Lilian. 2014. 'Kant's Not So Logical Subject'. *Harvard Review of Philosophy* 21: 87–105.
Antognazza, Maria. 2015. 'The Benefit to Philosophy of the Study of Its History'. *British Journal for the History of Philosophy* 23 (1): 161–84.
Armstrong, D. M. 1960. *Berkeley's Theory of Vision: A Critical Examination of Bishop Berkeley's Essay towards a New Theory of Vision*. Melbourne: Melbourne University Press.
Atherton, Margaret. 1983. 'The Coherence of Berkeley's Theory of Mind'. *Philosophy and Phenomenological Research* 43: 389–400 (reprinted in Walter Creery (ed.), 1991, vol. III, 336–46).
Atherton, Margaret. 1990. *Berkeley's Revolution in Vision*. Ithaca, NY: Cornell University Press.

Atherton, Margaret. 1997. 'How to Write the History of Vision: Understanding the Relationship between Berkeley and Descartes', in David Levin (ed.), *Sites of Vision: The Discursive Construction of Vision in the History of Philosophy*, 139–65. MIT Press.

Atherton, Margaret (ed.). 1999. *The Empiricists: Critical Essays on Locke, Berkeley, and Hume*. New York: Rowan and Littlefield.

Atherton, Margaret. 2010. 'Berkeley's Last Word on Spirit', in Petr Glombíček and James Hill (eds), *Essays on the Concept of Mind in Early-Modern Philosophy*, 115–29. Newcastle: Cambridge Scholars.

Atherton, Margaret. 2020. *Berkeley*. Oxford: John Wiley.

Augustine. 1997. *The Confessions*, translated by Maria Boulding, edited by John Rotelle. London: Hodder and Stoughton.

Ayer, A. J. 1980. *Hume*. Oxford: Oxford University Press.

Ayers, Michael. 1991. *Locke: Epistemology and Ontology*, vols 1–2. London: Routledge.

Ayers, Michael. 2005. 'Was Berkeley an Empiricist or Rationalist?' in Kenneth Winkler (ed.), *The Cambridge Companion to Berkeley*, 34–62. Cambridge: Cambridge University Press.

Ayers, Michael. 2019. *Knowing and Seeing: Groundwork for a New Empiricism*. Oxford: Oxford University Press.

Ayers, Michael, and Maria RosaAntognazza. 2019. 'Knowledge and Belief from Plato to Locke', in Michael Ayers, *Knowledge and Belief from Plato to Locke*, 3–33.

Beck, L. J. 1965. *The Metaphysics of Descartes: A Study of the Meditations*. Oxford: Clarendon Press.

Berman, David. 1986. 'The Jacobitism of Berkeley's Passive Obedience'. *Journal of the History of Ideas* 47 (2): 309–19.

Berman, David. 1994. *George Berkeley: Idealism and the Man*. Oxford: Clarendon Press.

Berman, David. 2015. *ΨΦ Penult*. Dublin: Artisan Philosophy Workbooks.

Bernier, François. [1684] 1992. *Abrégé de La Philosophie de Gassendi*. Paris: Fayard.

Bettcher, Talia Mae. 2007. *Berkeley's Philosophy of Spirit: Consciousness, Ontology and the Elusive Subject*. New York: Continuum.

Bettcher, Talia Mae. 2010. Manuscript. 'Berkeley on Substance', presented at the Berkeley Society conference at Neuchâtel.

Bonk, Sigmund. 1997. *'We See God': George Berkeley's Philosophical Theology*. Frankfurt am Main: Peter Lang.

Bracken, Harry. M. 1974. *Berkeley*. London: Macmillan.

Bradatan, Costica. 2006. *The Other Bishop Berkeley: An Exercise in Reenchantment*. New York: Fordham University Press.

Brandt Bolton, Martha. 1987. 'Berkeley's Objection to Abstract Ideas and Unconceived Objects', in Ernest Sosa (ed.), *Essays on the Philosophy of George Berkeley*, 61–81. Dordrecht: Reidel.

Brentano, Franz. 1995. *Psychology from an Empirical Standpoint*. London: Routledge.

Browne, Joseph. 1975. *Berkeley's Intellectualism*. New York: St John's University Press.

Brykman, Geneviève. 1985. 'Pleasure and Pain versus Ideas in Berkeley'. *Hermathena* 139: 127–37.

Carroll, William. 1705. *Remarks upon Mr. Clarke's Sermons, Preached at St Paul's against Hobbs, Spinoza, and Other Atheists*. London.

Carroll, William. 1706. *A Dissertation upon the Tenth Chapter of the Fourth Book of Mr. Locke's Essay concerning Humane Understanding. Wherein That Author's Endeavours to Establish Spinoza's Atheistical Hypothesis … Are Discover'd*. London.

Clarke, Desmond M. 2003. *Descartes' Theory of Mind*. Oxford: Oxford University Press.

Clarke, Desmond M. 2008. 'Introduction', in Desmond Clarke (ed.), *George Berkeley: Philosophical Writings*, ix–xxxvi. Cambridge: Cambridge University Press.

Collins, Anthony. 1715. *Philosophical Inquiry Concerning Human Liberty*. London.

Creery, Walter (ed.). 1991. *George Berkeley: Critical Assessments* (three volumes). London: Routledge.

Daniel, Stephen. 2001. 'Berkeley's Christian Neoplatonism, Archetypes and Divine Ideas'. *Journal of the History of Ideas* 39 (2): 239–58.

Daniel, Stephen. 2010. 'How Berkeley's Works Are Interpreted', in Silvia Parigi (ed.) *George Berkeley: Religion and Science in the Age of Enlightenment*, 3–14. Dordrecht: Springer.

Daniel, Stephen. 2013. 'Berkeley's Doctrine of Mind and the "Black List Hypothesis": A Dialogue'. *Southern Journal of Philosophy* 51 (1): 24–41.

Daniel, Stephen. 2018. 'Berkeley's Non-Cartesian Notion of Spiritual Substance'. *Journal of the History of Philosophy* 56 (4): 659–82.

Daniel, Stephen. 2021. *George Berkeley and Early Modern Philosophy*. Oxford: Oxford University Press.

Darwall, Stephen. 2005. 'Berkeley's Moral and Political Philosophy', in *The Cambridge Companion to Berkeley*, edited by K. P. Winkler, 311–38. Cambridge: Cambridge University Press.

Dennett, Daniel. 2005. *Sweet Dreams: Philosophical Obstacles to a Science of Consciousness*. Cambridge, MA: MIT Press.

Dicker, Georges. 2011. *Berkeley's Idealism: A Critical Examination*. Oxford: Oxford University Press.

Fichte, J. G. 1994. *Introductions to the* Wissenschaftslehre, translated and edited by Daniel Breazeale. Indianapolis, IN: Hackett.

Fields, Keota. 2011. *Berkeley: Ideas, Immaterialism, and Objective Presence*. Lanham, MD: Lexington Books.

Fischer, Kuno. 1897–1901. *Geschichte der neueren Philosophie*, 6 vols. Heidelberg.

Flage, Daniel. 1987. *Berkeley's Doctrine of Notions: A Reconstruction Based on His Theory of Meaning*. London: Croom Helm.

Flage, Daniel. 2004. 'Berkeley's Epistemic Ontology: *The Principles*'. *Canadian Journal of Philosophy* 34 (1): 25–60.

Flage, Daniel. 2014. *Berkeley*. Cambridge, MA: Polity.

Fodor, Jerry. 2003. *Hume Variations*. Oxford: Oxford University Press.

Fraser, Alexander Campbell. 1901. 'Prefaces and Annotations', in *The Works of George Berkeley*, vols I–IV, edited by A. C. Fraser. Oxford: Clarendon (reprinted by Bristol Thoemmes, 1994).

Frege, Gottlob. 1986. *The Foundations of Arithmetic* (second revised edition), translated by J. L. Austin. Oxford: Blackwell.

Fritz, Anita D. 1954. 'Berkeley's Self – Its Origin in Malebranche'. *Journal of the History of Ideas* 15 (4): 554–72.

Garrett, Don. 1997. *Cognition and Commitment in Hume's Philosophy*. Oxford: Oxford University Press.

Gassendi, Pierre. 1962. *Disquisitio Metaphysica*, edited and translated into French by Bernard Rochot. Paris: Vrin.

Geach, Peter. [1960] 1971. *Mental Acts: Their Content and Their Objects*. London: Routledge.

Glombíček, Petr, and Hill, James (eds). 2010. *Essays on the Concept of Mind in Early-Modern Philosophy*. Newcastle: Cambridge Scholars Publishing.

Grayling, A. C. 1986. *Berkeley: The Central Arguments*. London: Duckworth/Open Court.

Grayling, A. C. 2005. 'Berkeley's Argument for Immaterialism', in Kenneth Winkler (ed.), *The Cambridge Companion to Berkeley*, 166–89. Cambridge: Cambridge University Press.

Green, Thomas Hill. 1886. 'Introduction', in T. H. Green and T. H. Grose (ed.), David Hume, *Philosophical Works* (reprinted by Aalen: Scientia Verlag, 1964).

Gueroult, Martial. 1970. *Etudes sur Descartes, Spinoza, Malebranche et Leibniz*. New York: Olms Hildesheim.

Hamou, Philippe. 2006. 'L'opinion de Locke sur la "matière pensante"', in *John Locke: Critical Assessments*, series II, Peter Anstey (ed.), vol. III, 169–212. London: Routledge.

Hamou, Philippe. 2018. 'Locke and Descartes on Selves and Thinking Substances', in *Locke and Cartesian Philosophy*, Philippe Hamou and Martine Pécharman (eds). Oxford: Oxford University Press.

Häyry, Matti. 2012. '*Passive Obedience* and Berkeley's Moral Philosophy'. *Berkeley Studies* 23: 3–14.

Hart, Alan. 1970. 'Descartes' "Notions"'. *Philosophy and Phenomenological Research* 31 (1): 114–22.

Hatfield, Gary. 1986. 'The Senses and the Fleshless Eye: The *Meditations* as Cognitive Exercises', in Amélie Rorty (ed.), *Essays on Descartes' Meditations*, 45–80. Berkeley: University of California Press.

Hegel, G. W. F. 1896. *Lectures on the History of Philosophy*, translated by E. S. Haldane and Frances H. Simson, three volumes, London: Routledge & Kegan Paul.

Henrich, Dieter. 1982. 'Fichte's Original Insight'. *Contemporary German Philosophy* 1: 15–53.

Hobbes, Thomas. 1839. *The English Works of Thomas Hobbes*, vols I–XI, W. Molesworth (ed.). London.

Hobbes, Thomas. 2012. *Leviathan*, vols I–III, edited by Noel Malcolm. Clarendon: Oxford University Press.

Jaffro, Laurent. 2004. 'Le cogito de Berkeley'. Centres Sèvres: *Archives de Philosophie* 67 (1): 85–111.

James, Susan. 1997. *Passion and Action: The Emotions in Seventeenth-Century Philosophy*. Oxford: Oxford University Press.

Jesseph, Douglas. 1993. *Berkeley's Philosophy of Mathematics*. Chicago: University of Chicago Press.

Johnston, G. A. 1923. *The Development of Berkeley's Philosophy*. London: Macmillan.

Jolley, Nicholas. 1990. *The Light of the Soul: Theories of Ideas in Leibniz, Malebranche, and Descartes*. Oxford: Oxford University Press.

Jolley, Nicholas. 2013. *Causality and Mind: Essays on Early Modern Philosophy*. Oxford: Oxford University Press.

Kant, Immanuel. 1929. *Critique of Pure Reason*, translated by Norman Kemp Smith. London: Macmillan.

Kim, Han-Kyul. 2019. *Locke's Ideas of Mind and Body*. London: Routledge.

Lee, Henry. [1702] 1978. *Anti-Scepticism or Notes upon Each Chapter of Mr. Lock's Essay Concerning Humane Understanding*, Facsimile edition. New York: Garland.

Lee, Sukjae. 2012. 'Berkeley on the Activity of Spirits'. *British Journal of the History of Philosophy* 20 (3): 539–76.

Leibniz, Gottfried. 1962. *Philosophische Schriften*, series 6, vol. 6, The German Academy of Sciences (ed.). Berlin: Akademie Verlag.

Leibniz, Gottfried. 1948. *Textes inédits*, two volumes, Gaston Grua (ed.). Paris: Presses Universitaires de France.

Leibniz, Gottfried. 1998. *Philosophical Texts*, translated and edited by R. S. Woolhouse and Richard Francks. Oxford: Oxford University Press.

Leibniz, Gottfried. 1996. *New Essays on Human Understanding*, translated and edited by Peter Remnant and Jonathan Bennett. Cambridge: Cambridge University Press.

Leibniz, Gottfried, and Clarke, Samuel. 1956. *The Leibniz-Clarke Correspondence*, edited by H. G. Alexander. Manchester: Manchester University Press.

Leroy, André-Louis. 1959. *George Berkeley*. Paris: Presses Universitaires de France.

Lloyd, A. C. 1985. 'The Self in Berkeley's Philosophy', in J. Foster and H. Robinson (eds), *Essays on Berkeley: A Tercentennial Celebration*, 187–209. Oxford: Oxford University Press.

Lloyd Morgan, Conwy. 1923. *Emergent Evolution*. London: Williams and Norgate.

Luce, A. A. 1934. *Berkeley and Malebranche*. Oxford: Clarendon.

Luce, A. A. 1953. 'Berkeley's Search for Truth'. *Hermathena*, Homage to Berkeley: Commemorative Issue 82: 13–26.

Luce, A. A. 1977. 'Berkeley and the Living Thing'. *Hermathena* 103: 19–25.

Malebranche, Nicolas. 1997. *The Search after Truth*, translated by T. M. Lennon and P. J. Olscamp. Cambridge: Cambridge University Press.

Marion, Jean-Luc. 1991. *Questions Cartésiennes*. Paris: Presses Universitaires de France.

McCracken, Charles J. 1986. 'Berkeley's Notion of Spirit'. *History of European Ideas* 7 (6): 597–602 (reprinted in Atherton (1999), 146–52).

Mill, J. S. 1919. *System of Logic*, 8th edition. London: Longmans.

Mill, J. S. 1969. *Essays on Ethics, Religion and Society, Collected Works*, vol. X, edited by J. M. Robson. Toronto: University of Toronto Press.

Muehlmann, Robert (ed.). 1995. *Berkeley's Metaphysics: Structural, Interpretative and Critical Essays*. Pennsylvania: Pennsylvania State University Press.

Muehlmann, Robert. 1995. 'The Substance of Berkeley's Philosophy', in Muehlmann (ed.), *Berkeley's Metaphysics*, 89–105. University Park: Pennsylvania State University Press.

Newsome, David. 1974. *Two Classes of Men: Platonism and English Romantic Thought*. London: Murray.
Newton, Isaac. 1999. *The Principia: Mathematical Principles of Natural Philosophy*, translated by I. Bernard Cohen and Anne Whitman. California: University of California Press.
Nietzsche, Friedrich. 1990. *Beyond Good and Evil*, translated by R. J. Hollingdale. Harmondsworth: Penguin.
Nuovo, Victor. 2017. *John Locke: The Philosopher as Christian Virtuoso*. Oxford: Oxford University Press.
O'Connor, D. J. 1952. *John Locke*. London: Pelican.
O'Daly, Gerard. 1987. *Augustine's Philosophy of Mind*. London: Duckworth.
Pearce, Kenneth. 2017. *Language and the Structure of Berkeley's World*. Oxford: Oxford University Press.
Pitcher, George. 1977. *Berkeley*. London: Routledge.
Plotinus. (1964–84) *Enneads. Plotini Opera*, three volumes. Oxford: Clarendon Press.
Reid, Thomas. 1863. *The Works of Thomas Reid*, two volumes, 6th edition, edited by William Hamilton. Edinburgh: Maclachlan and Stewart (reprinted by the Thoemmes Press, 1994).
Rickless, Samuel. 2013. *Berkeley's Argument for Idealism*. Oxford: Oxford University Press.
Rickless, Samuel. 2016. 'The Nature, Grounds, and Limits of Berkeley's Argument for Passive Obedience' (online). *Berkeley Studies* 26: 3–19.
Roberts, John. 2007. *A Metaphysics for the Mob: The Philosophy of George Berkeley*. Oxford: Oxford University Press.
Russell, Bertrand. [1912] 1967. *The Problems of Philosophy*. Oxford: Oxford University Press.
Russell, Bertrand. [1946] 2004. *History of Western Philosophy*. London: Routledge.
Ryle, Gilbert. [1949] 1963. *The Concept of Mind*. Harmondsworth: Penguin.
Schmaltz, Tad M. 1996. *Malebranche's Theory of the Soul: A Cartesian Interpretation*. Oxford: Oxford University Press.
Schopenhauer, Arthur. [1818] 1969. *The World as Will and Representation*, two volumes), translated by E. F. J. Payne. New York: Dover.
Sergeant, John. 1697. *Solid Philosophy Asserted against the Fancies of the Ideists*, London (Facsimile edition, New York: Garland, 1984).
Shaftesbury, The Third Earl of. 2000. *Characteristics of Men, Manners, Opinions, Times*, edited by Lawrence Klein. Cambridge: Cambridge University Press.
Sosa, Ernest (ed.). 1987. *Essays on the Philosophy of George Berkeley*. Dordrecht: Reidel.

Stephen, Leslie. 1902. *History of English Thought in the Eighteenth Century*, two volumes, 3rd edition (1st edition, 1876). London: Smith, Elder, and Co. (reprinted by Thoemmes, 1991).

Storrie, Stefan. 2012a. 'What Is It the Unbodied Spirit Cannot So? Berkeley and Barrow on the Nature of Geometrical Construction'. *British Journal for the History of Philosophy* 20 (2): 249–68.

Storrie, Stefan. 2012b. 'Berkeley's Apparent Cartesianism in De Motu'. *Archiv für geschichte der philosophie* 94 (3): 353–66.

Storrie, Stefan. 2022. 'Berkeley and Irish Philosophy', in Rickless (ed.), *The Oxford Handbook of George Berkeley*. Oxford: Oxford University Press.

Strawson, Galen. 2011. *The Evident Connexion: Hume on Personal Identity*. Oxford: Oxford University Press.

Stumpf, Carl. 1939. *Erkenntnislehre*, two volumes. Leipzig: Johann Barth.

Thiel, Udo. 2011. *The Early Modern Subject: Self-Consciousness and Personal Identity from Descartes to Hume*. Oxford: Oxford University Press.

Tipton, Ian C. 1974. *The Philosophy of Immaterialism*. London: Methuen (reprinted by Thoemmes, 1994).

Tomeček, Marek. 2015. *Berkeley's Common Sense and Science*. New York: Peter Lang.

Urmson, J. O. 1982. *Berkeley*. Oxford: Oxford University Press.

Warnock, G. J. 1982. *Berkeley*. Oxford: Blackwell.

Weinberg, Shelley. 2016. *Consciousness in Locke*. Oxford: Oxford University Press.

Wilson, Margaret. 1979. 'Superadded Properties: The Limits of Mechanism in Locke'. *American Philosophical Quarterly* 16 (2): 143–50.

Windelband, Wilhelm. 1914. *History of Philosophy*, 2nd edition, translated by James H. Tufts. New York: Macmillan.

Winkler, Kenneth. 1989. *Berkeley: An Interpretation*. Clarendon: Oxford University Press.

Winkler, Kenneth (ed.). 2005. *The Cambridge Companion to Berkeley*. Cambridge: Cambridge University Press.

Winkler, Kenneth. 2011. 'Marvellous Emptiness: Berkeley on Consciousness and Self-Consciousness', in *Berkeley's Lasting Legacy*, edited by Timo Airaksinen and Bertil Belfrage, 223–50. Newcastle: Cambridge Scholars Publishing.

Woozley, A. D. 1976. 'Berkeley's Doctrine of Notions and Theory of Meaning'. *Journal of the History of Philosophy* 14 (4): 427–34.

Wright, John. 2009. *Hume's A Treatise of Human Nature: An Introduction*. Cambridge: Cambridge University Press.

Yolton, John. 1984. *Perceptual Acquaintance from Descartes to Reid*. Minneapolis: University of Minneapolis.

Index

abstraction, abstract ideas 38, 54, 62, 88–91, 93–96, 97, 99, 101, 102–3, 107–8, 114, 127, 128, 140 n.11, 147 n.60, 149 n.1, 150 n.3, 151 n.41, 155 n.33
Airaksinen, Timo 152 n.12
Antognazza, Maria 135 n.3
Aristotle 11, 13, 114
arithmetic 115–16, 119
Atherton, Margaret 139 n.5, 141 n.31, 148 n.11, 149 n.20, 149 n.38
Augustine 56–7, 144 nn.3, 5
Ayer, A. J. 4–5
Ayers, Michael 135 n.3, 145 n.16, 146 n.30

Beck, L. J. 144 n.6
Berman, David 7, 10, 111, 140 n.11, 152 n.23
Bettcher, Talia Mae 148 n.12
Bracken, Harry 11–12
Bradatan, Costica 135 n.30
Browne, Peter 125

Carroll, William 138 n.58
cause, causal power 1, 3, 31, 39–40, 43, 46, 54, 60, 62, 69, 72, 86, 110, 146 n.45
coincidence of opposites 11–12, 66
Collins, Anthony 21, 27, 148 n.18
concepts, conceptual thought 2, 31, 43–4, 60–1, 66, 86, 87–103, 107, 117–18, 119–29, 150 n.15

Daniel, Stephen 142–3 n.56
Darwall, Stephen 110
Descartes, René 3, 5, 7–8, 15–20, 21, 22, 23–4, 28, 29, 30, 35–7, 45, 47, 56–7, 59–61, 62, 66–8, 69–70, 71–2, 75, 77, 88, 90–1, 126–7
Dicker, Georges 143 n.68

dualism
  Berkeley's 7–9, 13, 48, 50, 75, 102–3
  substantial 7–8

emotions 19, 55, 56, 64, 100
empiricism, 4, 9, 11–12, 65–66, 70
  concept 7–9, 11–13, 21–3, 27–8, 32, 58–9, 65–6, 68–70, 102–3, 114, 119, 121–2, 125–7, 129, 134 n.15
  as paradigm of interpretation 4–7
ethics 105–14, 118, 129

Fichte, J. G. 70, 136 n.11
'Final Period' 10–11, 56, 76, 80–2, 85–6, 103, 105, 107, 109–10, 113–14
Fischer, Kuno 4
Flage, Daniel 6, 41–2, 134 nn.15–16, 141 n.31, 146 n.29, 153 n.25
Fodor, Jerry 150 n.15
Fraser, Alexander 10, 102

Garrett, Don 94
Gassendi, Pierre 5, 18, 59, 62, 66, 75, 126–7
Geach, Peter 144 n.70, 144 n.5
God 3, 12, 16, 23, 25, 26–7, 61, 64–65, 69, 90, 108, 119–29
good, the, 10, 55, 66, 89, 105–14, 118, 124, 129, 152 nn.18, 22
gravitation 112–13, 149 n.26
Grayling, Anthony 65
Green, T. H. 4, 5

Hamou, Philippe 139 n.63
Hegel, G. W. F. 4
'Heroic Period' 10, 11, 12, 55, 57, 103, 105, 107–8, 109, 134 n.25
Hobbes, Thomas 2, 5, 16, 19, 20–3, 27–8, 29, 31, 32, 33, 35–7, 39, 45, 46, 47, 50, 59, 62, 97–8, 127
Hume, David 3, 5, 9, 39, 48–50, 93–6, 114, 142 n.56

ideas 2, 5–6, 7–8, 10–13, 16–20, 22–7, 28–32, 35–54, 58–9, 62–3, 66–70, 74–5, 78–9, 83–4, 88–9, 90–1, 98–9, 102–3, 107–8, 110, 113–14, 116–19, 122–3, 136 n.26, 138 n.49, 142–3 n.56, 149 n.38, 150 n.3
immaterialism 1, 50–1, 84, 142 n.45
innatism/innate ideas 9, 11–13, 44, 55–70, 90, 91, 102, 119, 121, 125–7, 129, 145 n.15, 145–6 n.26
inner/internal sense 2, 12, 31, 66, 67, 109, 128
intellectual intuition 45, 70

James, Susan 56
Jesseph, Douglas 153 n.2
Johnston, G. A. 134 n.29
Jolley, Nicholas 136 n.26, 145 n.26

Kant, Immanuel 68, 81–2, 100–2, 108, 151 n.39
Kim, Han-Kyul 138 n.58, 139 n.62

language 21–2, 36, 52–4, 91–2, 96–9
Leibniz, G. W. 5, 60–4, 65, 66–8, 147 n.48
Locke, John 2, 3, 4, 5, 9, 15, 21, 27–33, 35, 36–7, 38, 39, 41, 46, 50, 53–4, 55, 56–8, 59–60, 62, 63–4, 66, 67–8, 77, 88–91, 107, 109, 114, 116, 121–5, 126–7
Luce, A. A. 25–6, 155 n.33

Malebranche, Nicolas 15, 23–7, 35–6, 39, 46, 61, 69, 91, 124, 136–7 n.26, 139 n.3, 140 n.14, 146 n.28
master argument 50–2, 65
McCracken, Charles 74–5
'Middle Period' 10–11, 44, 55, 100, 109
Mill, J. S. 70, 111
mind/spirit 10–11, 13, 15–20, 28–31, 35–54, 84–5, 118–19, 124

Newsome, David 135 n.32
nominalism 96–9
notions, doctrine of 1–3, 6, 9, 11, 21, 43–4, 49, 55, 62, 64, 67, 69–79, 102–3, 105, 115, 119, 129

number 7, 31, 44, 79–82, 86, 90, 105, 115–19, 129

particles (linguistic) 53–4, 58
Pearce, Kenneth 52
perception 9, 12–13, 16–20, 23, 24–6, 28–30, 42–4, 46–50, 51, 66–8, 90–1, 109, 112, 119, 129
  sense 28–9, 31, 47–8, 71–86, 91, 101
Pitcher, George 7, 41–2
Plato, Platonism 6, 11, 13, 39, 44, 63, 65, 69, 106, 110
Plotinus 135 n.31
pure intellect 5, 8, 17, 23, 24, 29, 56–7, 67, 70, 88, 90, 102, 108, 127–9, 155 n.33

rationalism 9, 69, 70
Reid, Thomas 5
relations 10, 44, 89, 100–3
Rickless, Samuel 110–11, 152 nn.18, 19
Roberts, John Russell 8, 128
Russell, Bertrand 4
Ryle, Gilbert 67, 74, 99–100

Schmaltz, Tad 136–7 n.26
self 2, 12, 15–54, 58, 61, 64–9, 70, 79, 84–6, 114, 120, 126–7
sens intime 66, 147 n.49
sense perception *see* perception
Shaftesbury, The Third Earl of 109
simplicity, simple ideas 38–9, 44, 48–9, 56, 81–2, 88–9, 113–14, 116, 118, 119, 122–5, 129, 140 n.11, 150 n.3
Spinoza, Benedict 5, 21, 135 n.4
spirit *see* mind
Storrie, Stefan 134 n.25, 154 n.26
substance 1–2, 3, 5, 7–9, 11–12, 21, 31–3, 43, 55, 60, 62, 64–7, 69, 116, 118–19, 124, 137 n.37

Tipton, Ian 141 nn.37, 39
Toland, John 21, 27
Tomeček, Marek 142 n.45
transcendentals 105
Two-Component View 72–4, 82–4

unity 1, 12, 31, 44, 55, 66, 78–82, 83, 87–8, 103, 113–14, 115–19, 123
Urmson, J. O.
utilitarianism 110–12, 152 n.18, 153 n.25

virtue 55, 64, 107–8, 109–10, 128

Weinberg, Shelley 138 n.49
Windelband, Wilhelm 4
Winkler, Kenneth 44–5
Woozley, A. D. 52–3

www.ingramcontent.com/pod-product-compliance
Lightning Source LLC
Chambersburg PA
CBHW061837300426
44115CB00013B/2419